Praise for

Not Drinking Tonight: The Workbook

"A beautiful follow-up to her previous book, *Not Drinking Tonight: The Workbook* is a compassionate and thoughtful guide for supporting clients as they navigate the often-daunting work of addiction recovery. With her personable and non-shaming approach, Amanda provides the language that clinicians need to help clients explore their relationship with alcohol, set better boundaries, and avoid falling into old patterns of behavior—all in service of creating a richly rewarding life."

—**Nedra Glover Tawwab, LCSW,** therapist and author of *Set Boundaries, Find Peace* and *Drama Free*

"So many people struggle with 'problem drinking,' and it can be a gray area for clinicians and clients alike. With its accessible harm reduction approach, not only does this workbook provide tools that help with making better choices, but many of the worksheets and exercises go beyond just drinking and facilitate overall well-being. This is a useful book for people seeking a self-help tool, as well as for clinicians seeking a guide for therapeutic work."

—**Ramani Durvasula, PhD,** clinical psychologist and author of *Should I Stay or Should I Go?*

"*Not Drinking Tonight: The Workbook* is the guide I was searching for as a new therapist. This workbook is filled with useful, targeted interventions that can be utilized immediately. Most workbooks are strictly focused on extreme cases of substance use and addiction. This one has tools that can be used by clinicians at the highest level of care and when working with people who are simply re-evaluating their relationship with alcohol. I highly recommend this workbook and believe it is a vital tool for clinicians working with a wide array of therapeutic concerns."

—**Whitney Hawkins Goodman, LMFT,** author of *Toxic Positivity* and owner of The Collaborative Counseling Center

"Amanda does such an incredible job of providing the most effective action steps for clients who are looking to build a sober life and examine their relationship with alcohol. The actionable worksheets in this workbook are wonderful tools that I use in session and that my clients work on at home. Amanda includes an array of practical strategies that focus on the client's specific goals while helping them learn how to regulate their emotions without alcohol. This guide helps create a wonderful toolkit for people working on their sobriety."

—**Alison K. Seponara, MS, LPC,** author of *The Anxiety Healer's Guide*, host of *The Anxiety Chicks*, and founder of The Anxiety Healing School

Not Drinking Tonight

The Workbook

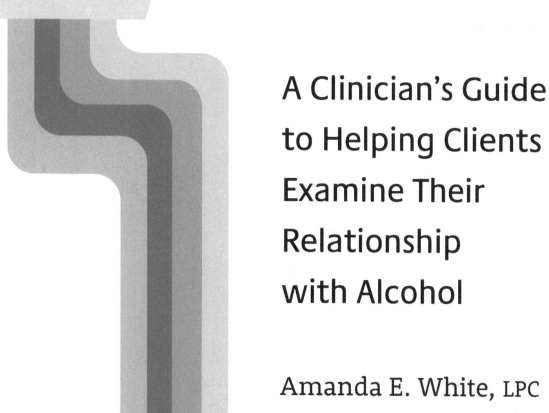

A Clinician's Guide
to Helping Clients
Examine Their
Relationship
with Alcohol

Amanda E. White, LPC

Published by
PESI Publishing, Inc.
3839 White Ave
Eau Claire, WI 54703

Cover Design: Emily Dyer
Editing: Jenessa Jackson, PhD
Layout: Emily Dyer

ISBN: 9781683735519 (print)
ISBN: 9781683735526 (ePUB)
ISBN: 9781683735533 (ePDF)

PESI Publishing
pesipublishing.com

About the Author

Amanda E. White, LPC, is a licensed therapist specializing in substance use disorders and the creator of the popular Instagram account @therapyforwomen. She is the founder and owner of the Therapy for Women Center, a group therapy practice based in Philadelphia serving clients across the country. People are drawn to Amanda's unique expertise and accessible approach to healing and mental health. She is the author of the book *Not Drinking Tonight: A Guide to Creating a Sober Life You Love* and has been featured in notable publications such as *Forbes*, *The Washington Post*, *Shape*, *Women's Health* magazine, and more.

Table of Contents

Acknowledgments

I want to start out by acknowledging the amazing team at PESI Publishing. To my editors, Kate Sample and Jenessa Jackson, what an honor it was to have editors who are also licensed therapists. You made this book so much more than I ever dreamed possible. Special thanks to my agent, Laura Lee Mattingly, who supported me throughout this process. I also want to shout out my previous supervisors, who taught me so much about therapy and supervision, in addition to the entire team at Therapy for Women. I learn so much from you all daily. To my friends and family, thank you for always supporting and believing in me. And finally, to my husband, who truly embodies what it is to be a partner, I couldn't do any of this without you.

Introduction

"I don't have a problem though. I've gone months without drinking," I protest. It is 2013, and I am sitting in my therapist's office.

On the outside, I didn't look like I had a problem. I didn't drink every day; I never went to the hospital or jail. I never went to rehab. My drinking was like Russian roulette. Sure, most times I drank, things were fine. But when I did drink too much and lost control, I had the tendency to become self-destructive. I would get into huge fights and say terrible things that I didn't mean. I would ditch friends and disappear from bars without a trace. I would drive drunk. All while I was in graduate school to become a therapist myself and (here's the kicker) I was an intern at a drug and alcohol rehab facility.

"Then taking a 30-day break should be no problem for you," she deadpans. As I shift uncomfortably, the leather couch sticks to the backs of my legs.

"Fine," I sigh. But in my head, I'm thinking, *Yeah, I'll do it. Because you're wrong. I don't have a problem. This will prove it.* Spoiler alert: I didn't prove her wrong. It took many more conversations and failed attempts at trying to moderate before I became sober. But this conversation was a crucial turning point for me. It helped me realize that just because I wasn't sure I fit the criteria for being an "alcoholic" didn't mean that I should keep drinking. I wanted to get better. I needed to get better. So I started attending Alcoholics Anonymous (AA) meetings and learned that abstinence-based programs were the only real form of treatment. I got sober and my life transformed. In my addiction classes, we were taught that people were either alcoholics who had a brain disease that would kill them, or they weren't. There was no in-between. This belief system was only further cemented when I went to work at a long-term drug and alcohol rehab program after completing my master's degree, where we were taught that harm reduction was dangerous. I met these viewpoints with skepticism and wondered if I *really* would have died if I continued drinking. But each time this skepticism crossed my mind, I quickly wrote it off as denial.

A few years later, I opened my own private practice in Philadelphia, and I was shocked to discover how many of my clients had issues with alcohol. However, none of these individuals were coming to see me for "alcohol addiction" or their inability to stop drinking. They ended up on my couch because they were depressed or anxious, had eating disorders, struggled with low self-esteem, didn't get along with their families, kept dating the wrong people, wanted more meaningful friendships, felt unfulfilled in their careers, or were going through any number of other things that seemed to have nothing to do with alcohol or addictive behavior—except, I realized, they do. Coming to this realization caused me to have a little bit of a breakdown, as I had to recalibrate my understanding of myself and my work as a therapist. My clients were not interested in going to AA meetings or quitting completely. Many barely met criteria for a mild alcohol use disorder. How was I supposed to help them? This workbook is my answer to that question.

In my work with these various clients, I discovered that it was easier for me to talk to them about almost any issue *except* their alcohol use. Why? Because of the stigma associated with alcohol use disorders. To my surprise, even talking about eating disorders was simpler. I could talk about their restricting, binging, or purging behaviors without them assuming that I was going to diagnose them with an eating disorder. Part of this is because there is a concept called "disordered eating," wherein an individual displays *some* characteristics and symptoms of an eating disorder but does not meet all criteria. This led me to come up with my own term for problematic alcohol use—disordered drinking—where someone meets some criteria for an alcohol use disorder (but not all), or they go through a period in their life where their drinking habits are unhealthy (like college). This puts them at risk for developing an alcohol use disorder in the future, but with early intervention and education, we can prevent it from advancing.

Approaching my clients' alcohol use through the lens of disordered drinking opened the door for me to help them without labeling them as an "alcoholic" or "someone with alcohol use disorder." This approach is counter to the dominant method of treatment, which unfortunately assumes that you either are an alcoholic or you're not—and that you are supposed to wait until you hit rock bottom before you can get help. But I don't think it's that binary. I believe that we are *all* capable of developing an alcohol use disorder or addiction, given the right circumstances, life stressors, trauma, or physical or mental health struggles. We need to stop othering individuals with the term *alcohol use disorders*. We need language to help clients examine their relationship with alcohol without feeling pressured to admit that they are an alcoholic.

In this workbook, clinicians will find these very tools—the tools they need to help clients pivot away from the question "Am I an alcoholic?" and consider instead "Would my life be better without alcohol?" I have a unique perspective on this issue because of my personal and professional experiences with alcohol. Not only am I someone who has been sober for over eight years, but I have experienced different periods in my life where my alcohol use met criteria for mild, moderate, and severe alcohol use disorder. I worked in the addiction field for many years using traditional methods before I branched out on my own and discovered the importance of harm reduction and more holistic approaches.

While this workbook is aimed at clinicians, it is a fantastic resource for anyone who is looking to change their relationship with alcohol. Simply disregard the word *client* and imagine that I am talking to you directly. Each chapter is accompanied by worksheets and exercises to help clients (or you) examine why they drink, stop drinking and stay in recovery, or change their relationship with alcohol over the long term. While these exercises can help clients make the choice to practice abstinence for a period, they are designed to meet clients where they are. Clients can complete most of the worksheets without ever cutting back on drinking. In fact, it can be helpful for clients to learn how to regulate their emotions, set boundaries, and engage in self-care before they are ready to change their drinking habits. The exercises are designed to wake up clients to the negative impact of their drinking habits (which can be destabilizing), while also stabilizing them with coping skills and tools.

Remember that you cannot rush the process of change. Just because you cannot see the change happening in a client's outward behavior does not mean that seeds are not germinating under the surface, getting ready to sprout. At the same time, this doesn't mean that you shouldn't refer a client to a higher level of care, if needed, or be honest about your observations. What it *does* mean is that you should avoid using shame or fear tactics as a means of forcing change (like many abstinence-based treatment methods). Instead, the most powerful thing you can do as a clinician is combine compassion with accountability, modeling to your clients how they can do this for themselves. I hope this book and my words support you in cultivating that balance. I also want to acknowledge that as a therapist reading this book, you probably spent your own money (and time) to read this resource on your off-hours so you can support your clients as best as you can. Thank you for being who you are in the world.

And one final note for individuals reading this book for their own self-help work: As someone who has been in therapy for most of my life, I know it can feel a little icky to read about what a therapist is thinking or doing behind the scenes. I remember when I first went to graduate school to become a therapist, I became worried that my therapist was only being "paid to care." It shook my trust. I want you to know that your therapist cares about you. Genuinely. They care, and their job is to help you meet your goals and work through patterns that are keeping you stuck. While not everything in this workbook will apply to you, it was also designed with you in mind. Use the tools in this book on your own or with the help of your therapist to gain an even deeper understanding into why you drink and how to change. I know questioning your relationship with alcohol can be daunting and overwhelming, to say the least. Thank you for having the courage to look at it anyway. You don't have to call yourself an alcoholic to question your drinking. You do not need to hit rock bottom. Rather than getting stuck in "Is my drinking bad enough to stop?" I encourage you to ask yourself, "Is my drinking benefiting me enough to continue?" Let this book be your guide to answering that question.

1

Would Life Be Better
Without Alcohol?

In therapy, clients have an opportunity to question their relationship with just about anything. They examine their relationship with their job, family, friends, upbringing, thoughts, emotions, environment, sleeping patterns, and everything in between. Therapy is powerful because individuals get to examine which of their beliefs and habits are serving them and which ones are holding them back from living the life they want. However, one area that clients often resist examining, and one that has big potential to negatively impact their lives, is their relationship with alcohol.

Alcohol is so tightly woven into the fabric of our lives that most of us have never taken a moment to question it. We use it to bond, to connect, and to commemorate almost every major holiday, celebration, and gathering. If someone says they don't drink, other people often assume that person is either an alcoholic or a social outcast because nobody in their right mind would voluntarily choose to abstain from alcohol. This creates a weird stigma where unless people have a *really good* reason, turning down a drink becomes synonymous with admitting they are an alcoholic. And in our society, if you ask someone what an alcoholic is, the word usually conjures up the image of an older man who—after getting several DUIs and losing his job and perhaps his family—spends most of his days drinking out of a brown paper bag on the street. Is it any wonder so many people avoid examining their relationship with alcohol?

I'll let you in on a secret: I don't care if your clients call themselves alcoholics or not. I don't care if your clients believe they have an alcohol use disorder. So often, clinicians get stuck trying to convince someone that they have a drinking problem before they even dig into the deeper reasons of why that person is drinking. Since abstinence is the dominant theory, clinicians are taught that breaking through someone's denial is more important than listening. Because 12-step programs are so interwoven with treatment centers, therapists learn that clients must accept that they are alcoholics before they can get better. If they don't, they may be labeled "resistant," and treatment becomes about breaking through their denial, rather than understanding their behavior. The truth is, a lot of work can be done whether or not a client believes they have an issue. Individuals don't need to accept that they have anxiety before you can teach them coping skills, and they don't need to admit to experiencing trauma before you can help them feel safe again. Focusing on whether or not someone is an alcoholic keeps people stuck as they spin their wheels trying to rationalize why they don't have a problem. Instead, the more important issue to focus on is whether a client's life would be better without alcohol.

According to the National Institute for Alcohol Abuse and Alcoholism, 26.45 percent of American adults admitted to heavy drinking in 2019,[1] with only 5.8 percent being diagnosed with alcohol use disorder. In 2020, during the pandemic, those statistics for heavy drinkers jumped to 34.1 percent.[2] Based on these numbers, it is clear that we leave millions of people out of the conversation. Instead of only focusing our efforts on clients who meet criteria for alcohol use disorder, we need to look at alcohol use on a wider spectrum. Clients need (and deserve) the opportunity to talk about their disordered drinking patterns and how it is impacting their lives without being stigmatized. Otherwise, the fear of judgment will cause them to hide.

When this judgment gets in the way, clients will minimize their issues and rely on Google instead of getting help. They'll desperately search "Am I an alcoholic?" and typically find comfort in discovering that they don't meet all the criteria on a specific list or quiz. *Whew! I dodged a bullet,* they might think. *No need to dig any deeper into my relationship my alcohol.* Sometimes these clients may decide to control their drinking or quit for a while, even if they don't directly admit that they have a problem. But most clients who have struggled with alcohol use in their past will struggle with it again until they do deeper work to heal what causes them to use alcohol as a coping mechanism. That's because alcohol use is a surface level behavior that only represents a small portion of what they are truly going through.

As a clinician, it can be challenging to identify when to bring up the issue of alcohol if it is not a client's presenting issue. Here are a few questions I recommend asking to get an idea of what their alcohol use is like and how it may be impacting their life:

- What does your relationship with alcohol look like?

- How often do you drink alcohol?

- How does alcohol positively impact your life? Are there any drawbacks?

- What is the relationship between alcohol use and your stress level?

- What are your friends' relationships like with alcohol?

- What is your family's relationship like with alcohol?

- What is your partner's relationship like with alcohol (if applicable)?

- Does alcohol play a role at your job? In what ways?

- How does alcohol impact your self-esteem?

You can explore these questions at the intake session or later down the road. If done during the intake, I suggest only asking the first four questions for data collection purposes, unless the client clearly meets criteria for alcohol use disorder or specifically indicates that they want to cut back on drinking. Alcohol can be a touchy subject for many, and it can damage rapport if you imply that your client has an issue with alcohol when they want help with something else. It can seem like you are hijacking the session with your own agenda.

Instead, I find that the most effective way to broach the subject is to help clients understand how alcohol is interfering with their goals or preventing them from living the life that they desire. This often requires waiting until the client brings up an issue they are experiencing with their friends, family, partner, or job. It may also require waiting until the client describes having a difficult night out after drinking too much. This provides an opening to examine how alcohol may be negatively impacting their relationships and their self-worth. As you probe into the client's drinking habits, it is important to refrain from using your own relationship with alcohol as a barometer. Some clients don't qualify as heavy or even moderate drinkers, but they *do* get into a fight with their partner every time they drink. Other clients drink a significant amount but end up just passing out on the couch. Focus less on how much they drink and more on how it impacts their life.

> ## Signs a Client May Benefit from Quitting or Cutting Back on Drinking
>
> - Drinking is negatively impacting their self-worth, harming important relationships, or preventing them from achieving their goals in life.
>
> - Drinking is impairing their ability to make progress in therapy or meet their mental health goals.
>
> - They are perfectionistic and have extremely high expectations for themselves. (Clients with these traits are often very sensitive if they act in ways that they later regret while under the influence.)
>
> - They don't always lose control when they drink, but when they do, there are significant consequences (e.g., losing friendships, fighting with important people, putting themselves or others at risk, putting their job at risk, or legal consequences).
>
> - They struggle with other addictive behaviors (e.g., eating disorders, chronic dieting, over-exercising, drug use, shopping, gambling, workaholism, codependency).

Remember that alcohol (or any other addictive pattern) is only a small part of what a client is really going through. A helpful way to understand this phenomenon is through the metaphor of an iceberg. Just like an iceberg, a client's symptoms reflect only about 15 percent of what is going on. Below the surface is the other 85 percent of the iceberg, which consists of two layers. The outer layer is made up of the more easily identifiable issues that may be contributing to a client's problematic alcohol use, such as anxiety, depression, low self-esteem, shame, fear, disconnection, cognitive fusion, and helplessness. Beneath that is the core layer, which comprises the more deep-seated issues that directly feed into the outer layer. This includes a history of trauma, a family history of addiction, a genetic predisposition toward addiction, environmental factors, and structural and systemic inequalities (i.e., in healthcare, housing, income, education) that the client has encountered because of their race, gender, ability, religion, sexual orientation, and class.

While this workbook focuses on alcohol, many clients struggle with other addictive behaviors, including drug use, dieting, disordered eating, gambling, shopping, workaholism, unhealthy relationship patterns, and perfectionism, that form the tip of their iceberg. Therefore, as you help clients work through this book, be on the lookout for addiction switching, or the whack-a-mole phenomenon, where every time they get one behavior under control, another pops up in its place. I see this pattern so often with clients once they improve their relationship with alcohol and stop drinking. Typically, it goes one of two ways:

The first is that a client feels so good about not drinking that they want to start cutting out any habit or pattern they believe is unhealthy or negative. While their motives might be in the right place, this quest often becomes sticky at best, as the goal of perfection is unattainable. At worst, they end up burned out with another addictive behavior that they must work on, such as chronic dieting, excessive exercising, or an obsession with "clean eating" (all the makings of an eating disorder). Sometimes clients even go so far as to become obsessed with tanning, Botox®, or other cosmetic procedures. The second pattern occurs when a person straight up replaces their drinking with another addictive behavior, like shopping, gambling, compulsive sex, self-harm, or drug use.

In either case, the client does not do the inner work needed to heal the root causes of their drinking. They simply find another habit or substance to fill the hole that sobriety has left. While they may be able to temporarily stay sober, most eventually go back to their preferred vice, whether that is alcohol or something else. Until you help clients heal the deeper part of the iceberg, they will always engage in some kind of unhealthy behavior, just like an iceberg cannot exist without some piece of it residing on the surface. Therefore, while the focus of this book is alcohol, know that many of the exercises in this book can also be used to help clients understand and transform other unhealthy patterns of behavior.

On the next page, you'll find a worksheet you can give clients to examine the intricacies of their own iceberg. The more areas under the surface they fill in, the more susceptible they are to developing an issue with alcohol or another addictive pattern.

Iceberg Theory

Think about your own addictive patterns of behavior (the tip of the iceberg) and what may be going on underneath the surface that is contributing to these behaviors. A sample iceberg is provided for you first, followed by a blank iceberg that you can fill in. Your iceberg won't look exactly like the example, so feel free to add your own ideas that are not listed.

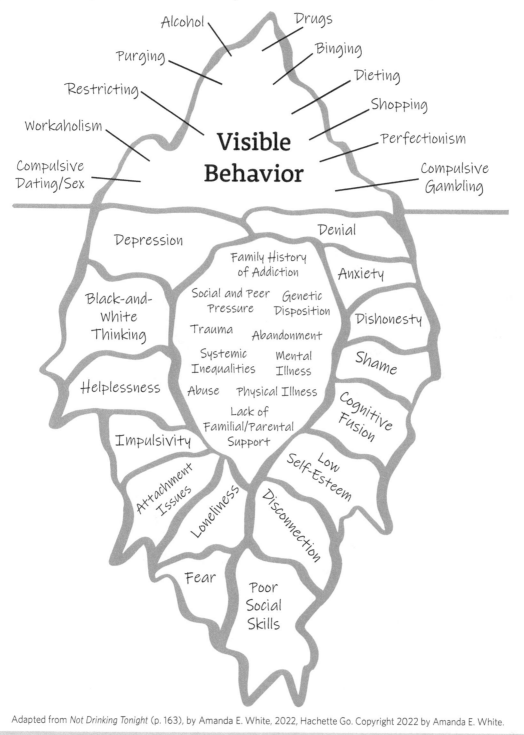

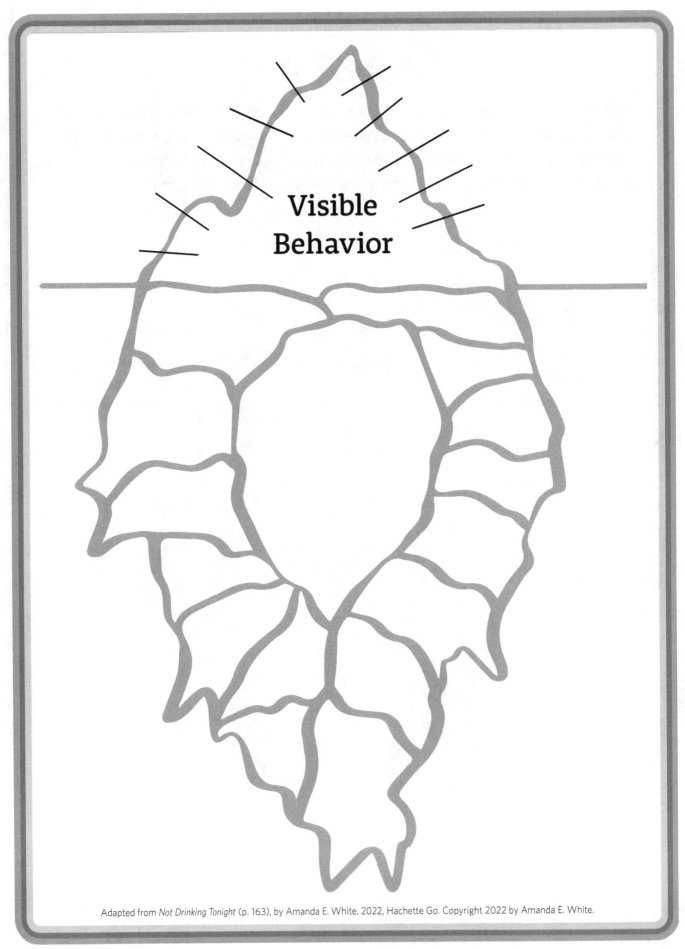

Visible Behavior

Alcohol History Inventory

When exploring a client's relationship with alcohol, it can be helpful to start at the beginning. Often, our first experiences with something lay the foundation for how we interact with it later in our lives, and alcohol is no exception. Sometimes those first impressions are hard to shake. Alcohol is an interesting topic because, for many clients, these impressions don't just involve their first drink, but their first memories with alcohol in general. For example, many of your clients grew up watching their parents or caregivers drink. The relationship that these trusted adults had with alcohol impacted your client's view of alcohol before they ever took a sip. In addition, just think of how frequently our society portrays people drinking on TV and in the movies. Whether your clients were conscious of it or not, these media messages likely impacted how they thought about alcohol too.

Alcohol History Inventory

Read through the questions below to consider how your relationship with alcohol first developed.

1. What are your first memories of alcohol? Did you watch the adults in your life drink? What did they say about their own drinking habits (or the habits of others)? Did you ever see them drunk or not acting like themselves? Did you ever try to sneak a sip of their drink? If so, what was their response? What emotions did you feel when you thought about being old enough to drink?

_____

_____

_____

_____

_____

2. Describe your first experience drinking alcohol. How old were you? Where were you? Who was with you? Was it your idea to drink or someone else's? Did you feel pressured to drink (whether directly or indirectly because you wanted to fit in)? What did you drink and how much? What was the emotional experience like? Did you enjoy it? Did you get drunk? Did you get sick? Do you remember thinking about the future and if you would drink again?

_____

_____

_____

_____

_____

3. When you think about alcohol, what are the first few words you think of? Do you think of fun? Relaxation? Stress relief? Freedom? What do you associate alcohol with? Know that alcohol may bring up conflicting associations for you as well. For example, it may mean freedom but also pain or unpredictability. That's okay; list them here anyway.

_____

_____

_____

_____

_____

4. When you think about someone who doesn't drink or is sober, what are the first few words you think of? For example, do you think they are boring or incapable of having fun? Are they uptight? A loser?

_____

_____

_____

_____

_____

Alcohol Serves a Purpose

Everything your clients do serves them in some capacity, or they would not keep doing it—drinking included. Does this mean that drinking is healthy for them? No. Does this mean that they should continue doing it? Not necessarily. But clients would not continue to drink unless it was meeting a need or serving a purpose. Most clients have never thought about it this way. However, if you are going to support your clients in changing their relationship with alcohol, it's important to help them understand that their alcohol consumption, regardless of its negative impact, also provides a payoff.

This payoff is the reason that so many clients struggle with the concept of change in general, beyond just changing their drinking habits. For example, consider a client who is miserable at their current job but can't bring themselves to apply to other positions. In this case, there is likely a hidden payoff of staying in their current role. Even if they are miserable, it takes less energy for them to stay in a position where they know the ins and outs of the job than it takes to start from scratch somewhere new. They may also be protecting themselves from the possibility of getting rejected or being unable to find a new position, making it easier to stay than put themselves out there and fail.

Alcohol works the same way. For most clients, alcohol is a crutch that they come to depend on in some capacity. This doesn't mean that every client can't function without it or that they are *addicted* to it, per se. It simply means that many clients use alcohol to make their lives easier. For example, they may drink to ease the awkwardness of social anxiety, relieve stress after a long day, or gain the confidence to have a hard conversation with a friend. However, clients don't realize that they can develop the capacity to do all these things without alcohol. In fact, alcohol is not even that effective in these situations! Therefore, what you really need to do is teach clients how to work through their social anxiety, process their emotions, and set boundaries.

Physical Health

While alcohol is undoubtedly serving a purpose in your clients' lives, it is also important to educate them on the health impacts that even one serving of alcohol has on their bodies. Most of us know that heavy drinking is not good for us and can cause a host of diseases. However, it's rarely acknowledged that even one serving of alcohol can negatively impact our bodies.[3] It is important to know that alcohol, or ethanol, has the same chemical compound that is found in rocket fuel. The second alcohol is ingested, our bodies are looking to get rid of it as soon as possible. To do this, the body halts the regular digestion of food and essentially fast-tracks the digestion of alcohol so it can be eliminated via the liver. As you can imagine, this majorly disrupts the gastrointestinal system and limits the body's ability to derive nutrients from any food consumed while drinking. This is why alcohol consumption is linked to bloating, constipation, diarrhea, loose stools, cramping, and headaches.[4]

Alcohol also destroys good bacteria in the gut, causing an imbalance in our microbiome that allows unhealthy bacteria to flourish (a condition called *dysbiosis*). This matters because the bacteria in our gut produce neurochemicals, like serotonin and other neurotransmitters, that affect brain functioning. In fact, scientists report that gut bacteria are responsible for producing over 95 percent of the brain's serotonin.[5] Alcohol also messes with blood sugar balance because when we drink more alcohol than the liver can handle, it stops producing glucose and the hormones that regulate blood sugar levels. Clients who make it a habit to not eat much while drinking are even more likely to exhibit low blood sugar.[6] Over time, heavy drinkers can develop hypoglycemia.

If clients drink alcohol faster than their body can break it down and metabolize it, this causes further issues, such as broken capillaries and, ultimately, cancer. This is because the body is incapable of breaking down ethanol, so it turns it into acetaldehyde before breaking it down.[7] The World Health Organization classifies acetaldehyde as a Class 1 Human Carcinogen because it not only damages our cells, but it also prevents the body from repairing this damage, leading to the formation of cancer cells.[8] Since acetaldehyde is highly toxic, the body does not want to store it. The alternative solution is to release it through oxidation. In order to do this, blood vessels expand, which can burst capillaries. However, sometimes the body is unable to keep up and completely rid itself of acetaldehyde through oxidation, so it stays in the system, which is one reason alcohol can show up in people's breath and sweat.

In addition, alcohol can disrupt the production of hormones like insulin and estrogen, which can impact the rate at which cells divide, leading to cancer. Breast cancer is specifically linked to drinking. Over a four-year period, one study found that women increase their risk of breast cancer by 15 percent if they drink three alcoholic beverages a week, and it increases by 10 percent with each additional drink they have after that.[9] Alcohol has also been linked to strokes and Alzheimer's disease.[10]

Finally, many clients use alcohol as a sleep aid, but the truth is even one serving of alcohol completely disrupts sleep. While clients may think that alcohol helps them fall asleep faster, it merely causes an initial sedating effect that is similar to a mild form of anesthesia, as opposed to a state of natural sleep.[11] Thus, clients are not actually falling asleep faster; they are simply experiencing sedation. In addition, alcohol-induced sleep is not restful for two reasons. First, it results in fragmented sleep and multiple night awakenings, though this is often subtle enough to be unobservable by the individual experiencing it. Second, alcohol completely prevents the body from entering the most restful and important type of sleep: rapid eye moment (REM) sleep. REM sleep is crucial for learning, as it is during this part of the sleep cycle that the brain transfers short-term memories into long-term memory. And remember, the body takes a few days to completely rid itself of alcohol, so clients can experience a disruption in their sleep even a day or so after drinking alcohol. If a client drinks alcohol a few times a week, they may never get into REM cycle sleep because their body never fully rids itself of the alcohol in their system. Unsurprisingly, this can cause long-term health effects.

How Does Alcohol Impact Your Physical Health?

Read through the questions below to consider how alcohol may be negatively impacting your physical health.

1. Do you have any preexisting conditions that are exacerbated by drinking? This can include diabetes, liver disease, hypertension, epilepsy, and more.

   _____

   _____

   _____

   _____

2. Are you taking any medications that are less effective because of your alcohol consumption or that pose dangerous side effects when mixed with alcohol? This can include blood pressure medications, insulin, antibiotics, and various psychiatric medications.

   _____

   _____

   _____

   _____

3. How does alcohol interfere with your ability to take care of your physical health? For example, is it affecting your skin, teeth, digestion, diet, or exercise habits?

   _____

   _____

   _____

   _____

4. What is your cancer, Alzheimer's, and stroke risk? Have you or anyone else in your family been diagnosed with these types of conditions, which makes drinking more likely to negatively impact you?

_____

_____

_____

_____

5. How is alcohol affecting your sleep? Do you find that you are waking frequently at night? Chronically tired in the morning?

_____

_____

_____

_____

Mental Health

As a clinician, it is important to help clients understand that no amount of alcohol is safe for the brain. Given all of the adverse effects of alcohol on the body, this should not come as a complete surprise. However, the findings of a recent large-scale study bear this notion out. After studying the brains of over 25,000 participants, researchers found that alcohol can create up to a 0.8 percent reduction in gray matter over time.[12] Gray matter is critically important for memory, muscle control, emotion regulation, and sensory perception. While a 0.8 percent reduction in gray matter may seem like an inconsequential figure, it is four times the amount caused by smoking. This explains why clients with disordered drinking may struggle with agitation, attentional deficits, and memory loss. Lead researcher of the study Anya Topiwala says, "There is no threshold drinking for harm—any alcohol is worse. Pretty much the whole brain seems to be affected—not just specific areas as previously thought."[13]

Like all other drugs, alcohol is an artificial chemical that stimulates the pleasure receptors in the brain. Since it results in an artificial high, and the brain wants to retain homeostasis, it produces chemicals such as dynorphin to reduce the intensity of this pleasurable sensation over time.[14] This effect is known as tolerance, and it's the reason why clients need to drink more alcohol over time to experience the same effects. However, these chemical effects also reduce clients' ability to find joy in non-alcohol-related pleasures.[15] If you've ever had a client who struggled to find meaning in their life outside of alcohol, this explains part of the equation. Drinking makes the ordinary moments in life feel less pleasurable, and it is these ordinary moments that are often cited as the key to living a fulfilling life.

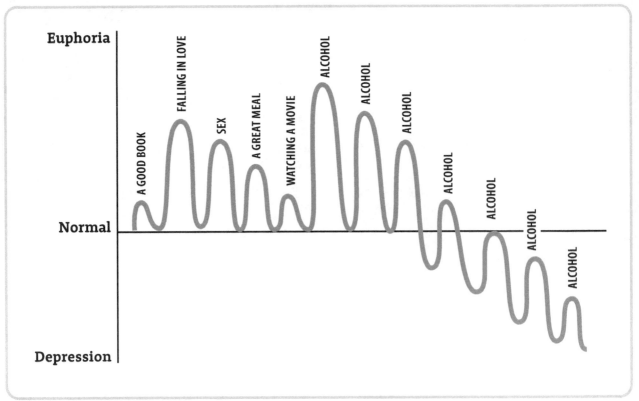

Alcohol also negatively impacts mental health due to the rebound anxiety it can cause. The human body always wants to be in homeostasis, so when a client ingests a depressant like alcohol, the body produces cortisol and adrenaline to counteract the effects of alcohol and bring them back to balance. Because cortisol and adrenaline are both stress hormones, this creates rebound anxiety as the body goes into a withdrawal state. This is true of any drug, not just alcohol, as withdrawal symptoms are always the exact opposite of the drug's effects. Drugs that make us feel relaxed (e.g., alcohol, marijuana, heroin) cause anxiety during withdrawal. Drugs that make us feel alert and awake (e.g., cocaine, Adderall, methamphetamines) result in an energy crash during withdrawal.[16]

It's important to know that at a physiological level, clients experience withdrawal even if they are not physically addicted to alcohol. The word *withdrawal* simply defines the process of detoxification that occurs as the body rids itself of what has been ingested in order to return to homeostasis. That means even clients who do not meet criteria for alcohol use disorder can experience anxiety and tension as their body detoxes from alcohol. This is extremely important for clients to understand, as a huge majority will experience anxiety (or "hangxiety" as people call it these days) and have no idea that it is a physiological process they cannot control or mitigate. For clients who use alcohol as a coping mechanism, this leaves them with more stress and anxiety than they started with. Drinking doesn't alleviate anxiety; it merely sedates its impact. This isn't even mentioning that it's difficult for clients to take care of their mental health and build self-worth if they are continuously acting in ways that are out of alignment with their values when they drink.

How Does Alcohol Impact Your Mental Health?

Read through the questions below to consider how alcohol is negatively impacting your mental health.

1. Do you have any mental health disorders such as anxiety or depression? If so, how has alcohol affected your symptoms? For example, does it worsen your mood the next day or make you feel more on edge?

_____

_____

_____

2. Have you used alcohol to cope with any traumatic events in your life? If so, how has alcohol affected your trauma symptoms? For example, has your alcohol use ever triggered a flashback? Have you drunk to numb how you feel, only to feel worse later or the next day?

_____

_____

_____

3. Has your alcohol use ever caused you to traumatize or re-traumatize yourself? For example, have you ever ended up in an unsafe situation while intoxicated that you would not have if you were sober? Have you ever been in an environment or around people who trigger you because you were drinking?

_____

_____

_____

4. Do you use alcohol to manage your emotions? For example, do you drink when you're feeling anxious, angry, overwhelmed, scared, or sad?

_____

_____

_____

5. Do you ever drink alone? Why? What is the connection between feeling lonely and consuming alcohol?

_____

_____

_____

6. How does it feel to wake up after a night of drinking? What emotions do you feel the next day? Do you often feel regret about how you acted while drunk? How long do these feelings last? Do you often make promises to yourself that you will "never drink again" or "never get this drunk again"? How long do these promises last?

_____

_____

_____

7. What does it feel like to break promises to yourself?

_____

_____

_____

Alcohol and Relationships

The negative effects of alcohol are not limited to a client's own physical and mental health. Alcohol has ripple effects that permeate out into the world—impacting almost every relationship that a client has in their life. Although many clients feel like drinking is a way for them to develop closer relationships with people (often because it eases their social anxiety or gives them a feeling of belonging), over time, alcohol often has the opposite effect. When clients continue to use alcohol as a means of connecting with others, it can prevent them from forming deep connections because their authentic self is not present.

In addition, alcohol makes clients more likely to say or do things that they don't mean because they lose their ability to think about the long-term consequences of their actions. It's for this reason that clients are more likely to get into arguments with loved ones when they're drunk versus sober. They also become less reliable and don't follow through on promises, which can erode trust as other people come to learn that the client is someone they can't rely on. These relational consequences can spiral further when clients spend increasing amounts of time socializing with individuals who drink in the same way they do, which isolates them even further from important relationships.

How Does Alcohol Impact Your Relationships?

Read through the questions below to consider how alcohol is negatively impacting your relationships.

1. How does drinking affect your relationships with your family, friends, kids, or other important people in your life? For example, does it impact your ability to be present with them? Do you feel like you can spend time with them sober? Do you ever break commitments or promises to them because of your drinking? Do you ever cause arguments or say things you don't mean when you are intoxicated?

_____

_____

_____

_____

_____

_____

2. What do people in your life say about your drinking habits?

_____

_____

_____

_____

_____

Alcohol and Work

For many clients, alcohol is a seemingly unavoidable aspect of their work lives. Many companies use alcohol (in the form of office happy hours or meetings over drinks) as a way for employees to bond, network, or blow off steam. Some employers even serve alcohol in their offices as a way to show that they are "cool" and don't take themselves too seriously. Many clients in these situations continue to drink out of fear that they won't be able to fit in at work or do their jobs effectively without alcohol—especially when it comes to people in sales, the food industry, construction, entertainment, nightlife, or the arts. Other clients feel like they need alcohol to keep up with the pace of work or deal with burnout, as is often the case for healthcare professionals, attorneys, and individuals in the finance field.

However, with increased alcohol use comes increased work-related consequences and lower job performance. Even if someone isn't at the point of being addicted to alcohol or drinking daily, their use can negatively impact their career. For example, they might show up at work hungover and be less productive, say or do things that are not appropriate around colleagues or at work events, and be more at risk for on-the-job accidents. These work-related consequences apply to stay-at-home parents too, who often use alcohol to deal with the stress, isolation, and monotony of child-rearing. If a parent is under the influence around their kids, they are more forgetful, more reactive, and less emotionally present. Just because someone does not have a traditional job does not mean their work is not impacted by their alcohol use. The same is true for clients who are in school—they can experience similar repercussions.

How Does Alcohol Impact Your Work, School, or Parenting Duties?

Read through the questions below to consider how alcohol is negatively impacting your work, school, or parenting performance.

1. How does your drinking impact your performance at work or school? For example, have you ever shown up to work or school hungover, been late, or missed a deadline because of your alcohol consumption? Have you ever been distracted, not given your full effort, or had to "phone it in" for the day because of your drinking?

   _____

   _____

   _____

2. Have your goals or values at work or school shifted to accommodate your drinking? If so, how have your goals changed? For example, perhaps you wanted to go back to school, run a marathon, or travel more with your family, but now you are more interested in spending your free time drinking.

   _____

   _____

   _____

3. Have you ever had a meeting with human resources or been disciplined at work or school because of your drinking?

   _____

   _____

   _____

4. What do your coworkers, bosses, teachers, or classmates say about your drinking habits?

_____

_____

_____

5. Has your drinking ever affected your parenting skills? For example, have you ever had to cancel playdates or leave your child on their own for food and entertainment because you were too hungover to parent?

_____

_____

_____

Making a Choice

After helping clients examine the various consequences that alcohol is creating in their lives, an important next step in treatment involves gauging their readiness for change. To do so, I always find it helpful to have clients create a pros and cons list of continuing to drink versus getting sober or taking a break from drinking. This can help them make a choice about what they would like to do about their current drinking habits, whether that involves making a change, continuing with the status quo, or deciding to punt the decision until another time.

For clients with moderate to severe alcohol use disorders, denial is a huge barrier that keeps them stuck in the same patterns of behavior. For individuals with mild alcohol use, it is often fear and stigma that prevents them from questioning their relationship with alcohol or being willing to cut back. Regardless of which camp a client falls into, real change is not created as a reaction to fear. Rather, the education and reflective tools provided in this chapter can help move clients in this direction. Many clients are unaware of the health impacts that even one serving of alcohol has on their bodies. Many don't think about how their drinking impacts them beyond increasing their probability of developing certain cancers or liver disease. When clients learn more about how alcohol is personally impacting them, both in terms of the payoffs and the costs, they can make an empowered choice that is more likely to stick.

Are You Ready to Take a Break from Alcohol?

It's important to know that whenever you are struggling to make a decision, you have a few options. You can try to change (quit drinking or take a break from it), continue with the status quo (keep drinking), or not make a decision right now. If you are in the third camp, you have every right to be there. Being on the fence is a perfectly reasonable place to be, and it's important to recognize that this is a decision too. However, sitting on a fence can be quite uncomfortable, so to help you get off the fence and decide, make a list of costs and benefits for drinking and not drinking.

	Costs	Benefits
Continuing to Drink		
Taking a Break or Getting Sober		

Are you ready to take a break from drinking? If yes, clearly define your "why" so that you can refer to it in the future.

_____

_____

_____

2

Trauma

The human brain and body evolved to do a few things: eat, breathe, drink water, sleep, go to the bathroom, and procreate. All other things that humans are capable of, such as running, jumping, hiding, hunting, and building shelters, evolved to better meet those basic needs. In addition, as humans evolved, they developed the capacity to form social bonds to facilitate their survival. In fact, our hunter-gatherer ancestors were highly social animals who lived in small groups of people. Without strong jaws, sharp teeth, or lightning-fast legs to protect themselves against predators like mountain lions and bears, their survival depended on cooperation. Therefore, it was extremely important for our ancestors to be liked and trusted by everyone in their clan, or they were at risk of being kicked out of the group, which meant almost certain death. It is for this reason that natural selection has shaped us to be highly invested in what other people think about us.

While evolution helped our ancestors better respond to dangerous threats in their environment, the "threats" that clients experience in modern-day society are typically not about life or death. Clients are no longer in danger of being eaten by a mountain lion. Instead, they are in danger of being called out at work, failing an assignment at school, or being embarrassed by their kid's meltdown at the playground. And how do the majority of people cope with the difficulties of everyday life? You guessed it: by drinking.

This should come as no surprise since alcohol companies tout their beverages as the cure for stress. While their specific taglines may differ, the underlying message is the same: Alcohol will make your life better. Feeling awkward on a date? Drinking will take care of that! Need to make new friends? Alcohol will help you bond with your peers. Struggling with parenting? Have some "mom juice" at the end of the day. It is no wonder that clients are led to believe that alcohol is the panacea for life's stressors. The problem is that alcohol does not truly solve any of these problems. It just gives clients a temporary feeling of escape, only to make them more anxious later.

The Invention of Stress

During the Stone Age, stressors existed, but stress was not a concept because it was so short-lived. Hiding from a mountain lion was certainly stressful, but the experience did not last more than a few hours. The lion either found and killed our ancestors, or they escaped, and the mountain lion found something else to eat for dinner. The stressor passed. However, in today's fast-paced world, people are constantly inundated with stressors from every angle. Although most of these stressors do not involve life-or-death situations, our bodies still react as though we are in physical danger. That's because humans are equipped with a built-in stress response system that mobilizes us to respond to life-or-death scenarios. Known as the fight-flight-freeze response, this mechanism prepares the body to respond to danger by running away from it (flight), attacking back (fight), or playing dead (freeze). Freeze is a last-ditch response that people often resort to when the source of the threat feels too overwhelming to flee from or fight against.

During the fight-flight-freeze response, the sympathetic nervous system triggers the release of stress hormones into the bloodstream, which initiates a host of physiological changes that increase the chance of survival. To name a few, heart and breathing rates increase to allow more oxygen to reach the muscles, vision and hearing sharpen, pain tolerance increases, and the body stops doing anything that is not essential to survival, such as digestion, to save energy. Once the threat passes, the parasympathetic nervous system takes over to allow the body to heal and return to normal, a process called *allostasis*.

However, in today's stress-filled society, clients don't ever truly have a chance to achieve allostasis. Whether they're getting stuck in traffic, working late to meet an upcoming deadline, or feeling overwhelmed by their endless to-do list, they are living in a constant state of sustained or chronic stress. As a result, their body never gets the memo that they are safe and that the danger has passed. Instead, they stay in a constant state of fight, flight, or freeze. Furthermore, their minds can replay stressful events and worry about potential new stressful events that may happen, causing the body to react with the same intensity whether the feared scenario is real or imaginary. According to trauma researcher Elizabeth Stanley, the human brain evolved to feel most threatened by stressors that are novel, unpredictable, and uncontrollable.[17] Unfortunately, most issues that we face today are exactly that. They are ambiguous and potentially dangerous situations over which we have little to no control (such as climate change, inflation, or developing a life-threatening illness).

In turn, many individuals turn to alcohol in an attempt to regulate their stress levels. For example, clients get into the habit of cracking open a beer at the end of the day to forget their work problems. Parents start drinking wine at 5:00 p.m. to deal with the chronic exhaustion of not having childcare while working full time. Young adults start drinking to fall asleep at night because it seems like the only way to drown out their worries about the state of the world. The problem is that drinking alcohol does not bring the body back into homeostasis. As discussed in chapter 1, it does the opposite by forcing the body to release more chemicals to metabolize and rid itself of the foreign substance, leaving clients even more depleted and unbalanced than before they drank. For clients drinking to deal with health issues, it makes these even worse.

How Stress Becomes Trauma

Trauma occurs when the brain gets "stuck" in a stressful event and the body is unable achieve allostasis. However, not all stressful events result in trauma, and an even lower proportion result in a diagnosis of posttraumatic stress disorder (PTSD). However, it is important to understand and remind clients that stress and trauma, though distinct, are located on the same continuum and can start with the same stressor.[18] For example, let's say clients A and B both get into the same car accident. Both are seriously injured. Client A is taken to the hospital, where she is met by her supportive and loving family. She has good health insurance and makes a full recovery with the help of physical therapy. Although she is initially shaken by the accident, she begins seeing a therapist and is quickly able to recover her sense of agency and get behind the wheel of a car again.

Client B, on the other hand, has much less support. She is a single mother who recently escaped an abusive relationship and has been working hard to make ends meet. When she is finally discharged from the hospital after three months of intense physical therapy, she must work even harder than before to make up for the loss of income during this time. However, she struggles with uncontrollable flashbacks of the accident that interfere with her ability to drive, causing her to miss even more work. She is unable to afford therapy because of her mounting hospital bills, so she starts drinking daily to as a means to self-medicate.

As these two examples illustrate, trauma isn't as much about what happens to clients as it is about their interpretation, understanding, and processing (or lack thereof) of the event. Trauma occurred for client B because she was unable to recalibrate and find safety. Instead, she faced an uphill battle in recovering from the accident at every turn. She never felt like she had agency over her situation and, in turn, was not able to process and work through it. Over time, clients in this situation can develop hypervigilant nervous systems, meaning that they become overly sensitive to triggers, and even seemingly minor incidents can send their nervous system into a state of dysregulation. This can cause the effects of the trauma to compound, as the longer someone is exposed to stress, the more difficult it is for their brain to work through it. It's also important to note that trauma does not have to involve something as significant as a serious car accident. Sometimes it's the seemingly subtle everyday difficulties, compounded over time, that have the biggest impact.

This Is All Trauma

- Emotional neglect
- Gaslighting
- Harassment
- Invalidation
- Poverty

- Bullying
- Chronic illness
- Medical trauma
- Racism
- Heterosexism

- Sexism
- Ableism
- Weight stigma
- Social isolation
- Parentification

Trauma Inventory

Most individuals who engage in disordered drinking have experienced trauma of some kind. However, trauma does not only involve the experience of abuse, natural disasters, or some other life-threatening event. Trauma is any deeply distressing experience that overwhelms you, makes you feel powerless, and shakes your sense of self. It is also not necessarily one event; trauma can be the compounded experience of small events that have accrued over time. This worksheet will help you uncover how the experiences in your life have affected you and potentially caused you trauma. Since this can be a difficult topic, please be sure to go slowly. Take breaks as needed and process your answers with your therapist after completing it.

1. Have you ever lost a parent, caregiver, friend, or anyone close to you? If so, what was it like for you? Do you notice any distinction between who you were before versus after?

   _____

   _____

   _____

   _____

   _____

2. Did your caregivers separate, get divorced, or leave when you were growing up? What was that experience like for you?

   _____

   _____

   _____

   _____

   _____

3. Have you endured any physical, sexual, or emotional abuse? Or did you watch a loved one or parent experience this type of abuse? Did you grow up in a home that had domestic violence? How did that experience affect you?

_____

_____

_____

_____

_____

4. Were you bullied or teased as a kid? Did you feel different from others when you were growing up? How did you deal with it?

_____

_____

_____

_____

_____

5. Did you grow up in a home where your parents were not emotionally available? Where you had your needs provided for, but your caregivers didn't take an interest in how you were doing emotionally? Or they weren't able to emotionally support you? If so, how did that impact you?

_____

_____

_____

_____

_____

6. Have you ever experienced racism, sexism, classism, harassment, homophobia, or discrimination? How does this impact how you live your life?

_____

_____

_____

_____

_____

7. Do you have a disability or chronic illness, or have you undergone any kind of medical trauma? Were you in any accidents or did you have any surgeries? If yes, how has this impacted you?

_____

_____

_____

_____

_____

8. Have you ever had a miscarriage or abortion or experienced infertility? If yes, how has this experience affected you?

_____

_____

_____

_____

_____

9. Did you grow up in poverty? If yes, what was that experience like? How does it impact you now as an adult?

_____

_____

_____

_____

_____

10. Have you ever experienced discrimination because of the size of your body or how it looks? If yes, how has this impacted you? Are there situations you avoid out of fear of being ridiculed about your appearance? If so, which ones?

_____

_____

_____

_____

_____

Alcohol Timeline

In order to understand how a client's trauma history may be connected to their alcohol use, it can be helpful for them to create an alcohol timeline, which connects their alcohol use to significant life changes, milestones, and events in their lives. This allows them to visually discover patterns in their drinking history. Often, clients do not realize that certain life events were difficult for them or had an impact on their well-being until they see that these events are linked to a change in their drinking habits. The timeline exercise also allows them to visualize how their drinking progressed over time. This can be helpful in working through a client's denial about the severity of their substance use.

When working with clients to create their timeline, I recommend starting with their birth and ending with the current date. They should draw lines above the timeline to indicate anything related to their alcohol use (e.g., their first drink, periods of abstinence or reduced use, relapses, increase in drinking, or other addictions if applicable). Then below, they should note any significant stressors or changes in their lives, along with developmental milestones (e.g., going to high school, moving, death, divorce, medical issues). Not all these milestones will be correlated with alcohol use. However, many clients are surprised by the connection that their alcohol use has to trauma and other life changes. It is a powerful exercise to have your clients discover the connection without you having to explain it.

For example, in the sample timeline on the next page, a client, Sandy, never made the connection that she started drinking soon after her parents got divorced. When I originally asked her how the divorce impacted her, she said it did not. But once she saw this on her timeline, she started remembering how much they fought, and after a particularly traumatic night, when her mom would not let her go visit her dad, she snuck a can of beer from the fridge. This realization allowed her to make additional connections and get a clearer understanding of how her relationship with alcohol use was directly correlated to her mental and physical health.

Alcohol Timeline

In order to understand how your alcohol use is connected to any trauma, significant life changes, milestones, and events in your life, it can help to create an alcohol timeline that looks at the chronology of your drinking through the years. Draw above the line to mark anything related to your alcohol use (e.g., your first drink, periods of abstinence or reduced use, relapses, and other addictions, if applicable). Use the space below the line to mark any significant stressors or changes in your life, along with developmental milestones (e.g., going to high school, moving, death, divorce, medical issues). An example is provided for you first, followed by a blank timeline to create on your own.

Sample Timeline

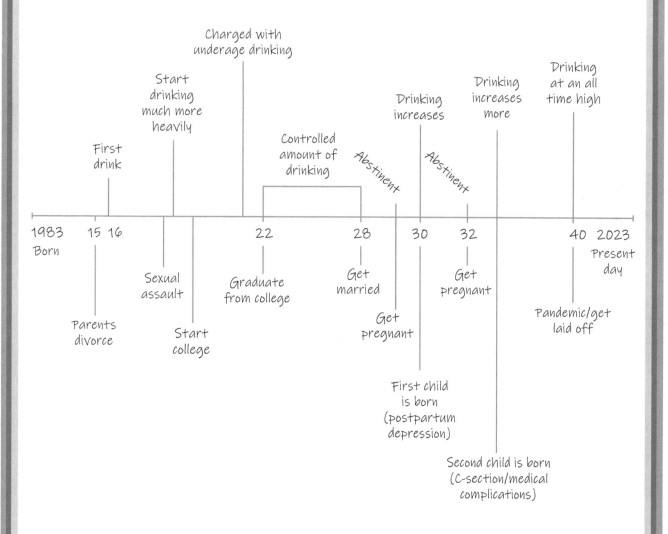

Your Alcohol Timeline

Alcohol Use

Today

Born

Stressors

Alcohol Timeline

1. What did you learn from this exercise? When you look at your timeline, are there any patterns you see related to your alcohol use and other milestones? Was there anything that surprised you?

_____

_____

_____

_____

2. When you think back to your history with alcohol use as well as trauma, is there a connection between the two? How have you used alcohol to cope with trauma or difficult stressors in your life?

_____

_____

_____

_____

3. If you have a history of relapsing, are there any patterns you notice? What often precedes a relapse?

_____

_____

_____

_____

Trauma and the Window of Tolerance

The window of tolerance is a concept coined by Dr. Dan Siegel that describes the state of arousal in which someone is able to function most effectively.[19] In other words, it is the state in which clients can handle everyday stressors without becoming triggered, anxious, or out of control. However, after clients have experienced trauma, their window of tolerance can decrease as their brain and body become hypersensitized to cues that they are in danger. Over time, this can cause them to spend significant time outside of their window of tolerance, in which they can quickly swing into a state of hyperarousal or hypoarousal in response to seemingly mundane stressors, like receiving a curt email from their boss or getting stuck in traffic.

In a state of hyperarousal, clients are hypervigilant, experience racing thoughts, and are overly reactive. They may constantly scan their surroundings for potential threats and be easily startled by sounds. Some common signs that your client is in a hyperarousal state include pressured speech, irritability, defensiveness, inability to sit still, hyperventilating, or jumpiness. Clients who survived trauma by fighting or fleeing from the source of the threat often present in a state of hyperarousal.

On the opposite end of the spectrum is hypoarousal, in which clients feel lethargic, disconnected, and shutdown. Common signs that your client is experiencing a hypoaroused state include emotional numbness (i.e., an inability to identify how they feel), disassociation, being zoned out, not speaking, slow movement or speech, shallow breathing, and blunted or flat affect. Clients who survived traumatic experiences by hiding from the threat or trying to appease their perpetrator often tend to lean toward states of hypoarousal.

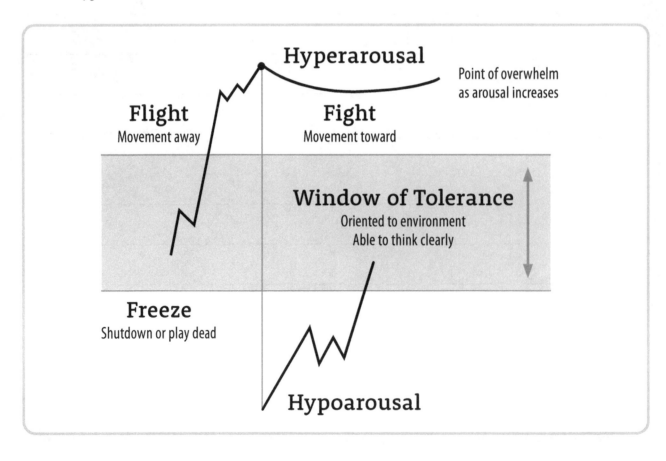

When clients are constantly outside their window of tolerance, drinking alcohol can become a way that they cope with this chronic dysregulation, as it numbs their emotions and thoughts. Alcohol is also a central nervous system depressant, so it literally slows down the nervous system if a client is in a state of hyperarousal and creates a temporary feeling of calm and safety. Although alcohol gives them short-term relief from their symptoms, it causes more dysregulation in the long term as their tolerance grows and they need more alcohol to create this sense of numbness. It also cuts clients off from their inner wisdom and ability to self-regulate. The more that clients drink, the more they teach themselves to feel disconnected when triggered. And the more they avoid their triggers, the more difficult it becomes to face them as they lose their ability to cope with everyday stress. As a result, their window of tolerance shrinks, and they are more likely to feel even more reliant on alcohol to find a sense of balance.

As a clinician, one of the most powerful ways to determine whether someone is outside of their window of tolerance is to notice their breathing. At the beginning of each session, get into the habit of noticing your client's breathing patterns. If they are breathing rapidly, unevenly, or taking shallow breaths, it is likely that they are outside of their window of tolerance. If so, it can be helpful to spend a few minutes taking deep, slow belly breaths together. The breath is one of the most powerful tools that clients can use to teach their body that they are safe.

Another helpful tip is to notice your client's eye contact and body language. If they are averting eye contact and displaying closed-off body language, they are likely outside of their window of tolerance. In this case, you can have them do some light stretches or a grounding exercise to bring them back into the moment and into their bodies. Your goal is to help clients regain a sense of regulation, as it is difficult for clients to make progress in therapy, gain insight, or retain what they learn if they are dysregulated.

In addition, it is important to teach clients activities they can do outside of session that bring them back into their window of tolerance. For example, if they are in a state of hyperarousal, encourage them to do activities that slow down an already revved-up nervous system, such as deep breathing, gentle stretching, taking a hot bath or shower, listening to soothing music, or resting under a weighted blanket. Some clients with hyperarousal have an excessive amount of energy, in which case they may need to discharge it by jumping, shaking, moving, or hitting a pillow before they engage in calming coping skills.

On the other hand, if a client is in a state of hypoarousal, they will need to engage in energizing and invigorating activities that wake up their nervous system, such as taking a cold shower, rubbing an ice cube on their skin, playing with a stress ball, chewing gum, smelling a candle or essential oils, or listening to upbeat music. Encourage clients to start with slower movement and then gradually build up to more vigorous movement as their nervous systems wake up and come back to the present.

Recognizing Trauma Responses

Trauma can push you outside of your window of tolerance, which is the state in which you can function most effectively in the world. Although it can be tempting to use alcohol to deal with stress or trauma triggers, self-medicating with alcohol actually makes you more likely to leave your window of tolerance, causing you to swing into a state of hypoarousal or hyperarousal. To take a break from alcohol or quit drinking altogether, it's important that you understand your signs of hypoarousal and hyperarousal so you can practice using alternative coping skills that bring you back into your window of tolerance.

Hyperarousal

1. How do you know when you are in a state of hyperarousal? This is the feeling you get when you want to fight or flee. Check off any symptoms that apply to you:

   ☐ Anxiety

   ☐ Panic

   ☐ Feeling on edge

   ☐ Paranoia

   ☐ Impulsivity

   ☐ Anger

   ☐ Restlessness

   ☐ Insomnia

   ☐ Irritability

   ☐ Being easily startled

   ☐ Racing or intrusive thoughts

   ☐ Inability to think clearly

   ☐ Defensiveness

   ☐ Obsessive behavior (rituals, counting, checking, etc.)

   ☐ Emotional outbursts

   ☐ Other: _____

2. What situations send you into a state of hyperarousal (e.g., being around your family, getting an email from your boss, walking home alone at night, being in a crowded bar, etc.)?

   _____

   _____

   _____

   _____

3. How do you normally behave when you are in a state of hyperarousal?

_____

_____

_____

4. The next time you find yourself in a state of hyperarousal, try using one of the following tools to regulate yourself instead of turning to alcohol or using another unhealthy coping skill. Put a check mark by any tools you are interested in trying:

☐ Shaking, stomping, jumping, or dancing out excess energy

☐ Hitting a pillow

☐ Slow, deep breathing

☐ Taking a hot bath or shower

☐ Stretching or restorative yoga

☐ Listening to calming music, chanting, or soothing sounds such as ASMR

☐ Going for a walk outside

☐ Being present in nature

☐ Lifting weights, doing pushups, or pulling a weighted rope

☐ Laying under a weighted blanket

☐ Drawing, painting, or engaging in a creative activity

☐ Eating or drinking warm or comforting foods or nonalcoholic beverages

Hypoarousal

1. How do you know when you are in a state of hypoarousal? This is the feeling you get when you want to disconnect or shut down. Check off any symptoms that apply to you:

☐ Depression

☐ Feeling numb or empty

☐ Inability to feel emotions

☐ Extreme fatigue or tiredness

☐ Memory loss

☐ Feeling like you are on autopilot

☐ Shame

☐ Defensiveness

☐ Absence of sensation

☐ Inability to say no

☐ Exhaustion

☐ Paralysis

☐ Difficulty engaging in basic tasks

☐ Dissociation

☐ Derealization

☐ Not feeling present with the world

☐ Other: _____

2. Which situations send you into a state of hypoarousal (e.g., being in certain environments, coming home at the end of the day, spending time with certain people)?

_____

_____

_____

_____

3. How do you normally behave when you are in a state of hypoarousal?

_____

_____

_____

_____

4. The next time you find yourself in a state of hypoarousal, try using one of the following tools to regulate yourself instead of turning to alcohol or using another unhealthy coping skill. Put a check mark by any tools you are interested in trying:

☐ Taking a cold shower

☐ Running an ice cube over your skin

☐ Splashing cold water on your face

☐ Applying lotion or a body scrub

☐ Lighting a candle or smelling essential oils

☐ Eating chewy or crunchy foods

☐ Doing vinyasa yoga

☐ Listening to upbeat music

☐ Dancing

☐ Playing with a stress ball

☐ Jumping on a trampoline

3

Shame and Self-Sabotage

Shame and guilt both play an integral role in influencing our behavior. Unfortunately, many clients do not understand the difference between these two emotions, which can keep them stuck, so let's break down the difference. *Guilt* is a feeling of unease or remorse that clients experience after they have done something wrong, especially toward another person. In this case, guilt arises because a client feels like their behavior does not align with their values or morals. In contrast, *shame* is a feeling that arises when clients feel like *they* are flawed as a person because of a behavior they exhibited. This is the critical difference between guilt and shame. Guilt is tied to our behavior, whereas shame is tied to our perceived worth as a human being. While guilt says, "I made a mistake," shame says, "I am a mistake."

Guilt can be a helpful emotion because it propels clients to take responsibility for their mistakes, apologize, and change their behavior in the future. However, shame is never helpful for creating true change. That's because shame leads people to question their character instead of their behavior. In turn, shame robs people of the ability to change because they get stuck in the belief "This is just who I am." The semantics of this may not seem important, but they are, especially when it comes to changing drinking habits. Most of the time, when a client relapses, they don't feel guilty. They don't think, *I made a mistake. I can get back on track.* Instead, they think, *I'm a drunk. This always happens! Why do I even bother trying? This is just who I am!* They use the experience as evidence that they cannot change, rather than recognizing that their actions are simply not in alignment with their values.

Of course, guilt can also become unhealthy or maladaptive, especially when it involves imagined scenarios that have not yet happened or are unlikely to happen. For example, a client may feel guilty at the idea of setting boundaries with a friend. They may also obsessively ruminate over their past mistakes and dissect everything they said or did in that situation. (This is especially the case when clients are trying to figure out if another person likes them or is upset with them.) Maladaptive guilt can also arise when clients set unrealistic expectations for themselves, especially if they struggle with low self-worth that gets further triggered when they inevitably can't meet those expectations. In this case, almost every mistake a client makes can become a source of shame (*I am a failure!*), rather than guilt. Therefore, it is important to understand the difference between shame and guilt because two people can make the same mistake, and one person may feel guilt, while the other feels shame.

The symptoms of shame can manifest in a variety of behaviors, such as perfectionism, codependency, avoidance, people-pleasing, defensiveness, shutting down, and self-sabotage. Let's say your client relapses or doesn't meet their goal of cutting back on drinking. Typically, they will react in one of the following ways if they are experiencing shame: (1) They will beat themselves up and turn their shame inward; (2) They will attempt to run away and hide; or (3) They will become defensive, maybe even angry, and blame others for their inability to stay sober. Let's break down what each of these reactions may look like. Though I am specifically giving an example of relapse, these reactions may also occur if you bring up concerns about a client's drinking or other situations pertaining to alcohol use.

When it comes to the first reaction, many clients struggle with perfectionism and expect themselves to be perfect with their sobriety. If they relapse, they go into a full-on shame spiral because they believe their slipup is evidence that they will never be successful. These clients may even beat themselves up for *thinking* about drinking. This is an incredibly slippery slope to go down. Clients cannot control their automatic thoughts, and it is difficult enough to change a pattern with an addictive substance, let alone expect themselves to never think about drinking. In these cases, it is important to reassure clients and help them check their expectations. Even years down the road, some clients may still have thoughts about drinking, but this does not mean they want to relapse or will. Instead, encourage them to view their thoughts about drinking as a warning sign, similar to a check engine light turning on in a car. It is an indicator that something may be off with their recovery, not that they are doomed.

The second reaction is characteristic of many clients who tend toward avoidance, as they often respond to the shame associated with a relapse by shutting down. They may become guarded and closed off in session, perhaps even denying that they feel shame or claiming that they no longer think alcohol is really an issue for them. They may isolate from others or hide the fact that they started drinking again, which only makes their shame worse. Some clients may even start canceling sessions or discontinue therapy altogether. In these cases, it is important to normalize how the client feels. You cannot force them to confront their shame, though you can explain why their reaction is making their shame worse and gently remind them of the reasons they wanted to cut back on drinking in the first place. Some clients won't be ready and may need to take a break from therapy before they are ready to work through their issues with alcohol again (either with you or with another therapist).

Finally, for some clients, shame will manifest through denial and defensiveness. They may get angry and blame you, the situation, their family, their friends, or their job for their recent relapse. They may claim that trying to abstain from alcohol or going to therapy is making them want to drink more. They may completely deny that they have an issue with alcohol. In these situations, it is important to remain grounded. Don't react to defensiveness with more defensiveness. Instead, model what it looks like to take accountability when confronted.

Regardless of how a client reacts when they are experiencing shame, it can be helpful to have them identify their specific signs of shame, including how shame may be connected to their alcohol use. To do so, you can have them fill out the corresponding "Do You Have Shame?" worksheet. Be sure to have them fill it out when they are in a good headspace, not when they are currently in a shame spiral.

Do You Have Shame?

Shame can be difficult for us to identify because, as a society, we don't tend to discuss it. Shame thrives in secrecy, so it's important to identify your shame before you can process and release it. Fill out this worksheet to see if you are experiencing shame in your life.

1. What does the word *shame* mean to you?

_____

_____

_____

2. Look over these common signs of shame and check off any that you experience:

☐ Perfectionism

☐ Avoiding people or situations that make you anxious

☐ Shutting down

☐ Isolating from others when you need support

☐ Keeping your problems a secret

☐ People-pleasing

☐ Catastrophizing

☐ Wanting to disappear

☐ Always blaming yourself

☐ Self-punishment or sabotage

☐ Anger

☐ Codependency

☐ Burnout

☐ Defensiveness or blame

☐ Never feeling good enough

3. How do any of these symptoms show up in relation to your alcohol use?

_____

_____

_____

4. Do you exhibit any of these behaviors whenever someone shares a concern about your alcohol use? (If nobody has ever brought up your alcohol use, imagine how you would feel if they did and how you might respond.)

_____

_____

_____

5. Do you exhibit any of these behaviors when you have relapsed or not met your goal of cutting back? (If this has never happened before, imagine how you would you feel if it did and how you might respond.)

_____

_____

_____

Humiliation and Embarrassment

Humiliation and embarrassment are two additional emotional experiences that are often confused with each other and with the concepts of shame and guilt. *Embarrassment* is a feeling of nervousness or self-consciousness that arises when someone is worried about what other people might think of them. This is a common experience that can happen when a client makes a mistake or brings unwanted attention to themselves.[20] For example, a client may feel embarrassed for drinking too much but is able to laugh about it with their friends the next morning.

In contrast, *humiliation* involves a painful loss of pride, self-respect, or dignity. This can happen when clients are called out publicly or labeled a certain name based on their behavior. For example, let's say a client is attending a family wedding where they try to drink responsibly but end up drinking to the point of intoxication. In response, their aunt snatches a drink out of their hand on the dance floor, calls them an alcoholic, and informs them that they need to leave. This client feels humiliated because their behavior caused a scene in front of the entire family. They also feel ashamed because they tried to moderate their alcohol use, yet it still got out of control.

However, a client can feel humiliated without feeling shame. When people are humiliated, their sense of pride is wounded. However, when people are both humiliated *and* ashamed, they also believe that they deserve what happened to them. For example, the same client could feel humiliated if they were to get into a bar fight and have a drink thrown on them, but they wouldn't feel ashamed if they believed the incident was the other person's fault. Therefore, as painful as it is to be humiliated, shame is a more damaging emotion. Nevertheless, the more often that a client is humiliated, especially by someone they respect and admire, the lower their self-worth. This can make them more susceptible to internalizing the humiliation, which can then easily turn into shame.

What Emotion Is It?

Guilt (including maladaptive guilt), shame, embarrassment, and humiliation are emotions that are often used interchangeably. The truth is these are distinct emotions. This worksheet will help you decipher times when you have felt these different emotions. Fill in the table below with an example of a time when you felt adaptive guilt, maladaptive guilt, shame, embarrassment, and humiliation. If applicable, use an example that is connected to your alcohol use.

Emotion	Definition	Example	Your Example
Adaptive guilt	The feeling of unease or remorse after you have done something wrong, especially toward another person	Tara feels guilty for being late to her doctor's appointment. She knows this is not like her and plans to leave earlier in the future.	
Maladaptive guilt	Feeling guilty over circumstances that are imaginary or out of control, or obsessively ruminating over a mistake or wrongdoing	Tara feels guilty about setting boundaries with her mom because she knows that her mom will take it personally.	
Shame	The feeling or experience of believing that you are flawed and therefore unworthy of love and belonging	Tara feels like a bad person because she has dropped out of college, has been to rehab numerous times, and keeps blacking out. She calls herself a loser.	
Embarrassment	The feeling of being nervous or self-conscious about what people think of you	Tara gets too drunk for the first time and is embarrassed that she made a fool of herself. She and her friends joke about this and move on.	
Humiliation	The painful loss of pride, self-respect, or dignity	Tara is called a "junkie" while she is in rehab for her problematic drinking, and she feels humiliated because she doesn't even do drugs.	

Shame and Trauma

Shame and trauma are inextricably linked. Since the hallmark of trauma is a feeling of powerlessness to stop or change the traumatic event, shame immediately sprouts up as a way to make sense of the experience. That means clients who have experienced trauma are likely to tell themselves, *It's my fault this happened. If I would have done or said this, I could have prevented it. I should have been able to stop it. I'm a bad person.* As Bessel van der Kolk states, "Deep down many traumatized people are even more haunted by the shame they feel about what they themselves did or did not do under the circumstances. They despise themselves for how terrified, dependent, excited, or enraged they felt."[21]

At its core, shame involves a fear of disconnection. If clients have been through something traumatic, they often fear that other people will abandon or reject them if they find out. Since people who have endured trauma often blame themselves for the experience, they assume other people do the same as well. So what do clients do to prevent that from happening? They hide their trauma. They pretend it didn't happen, don't talk about it, and judge themselves for the experience. However, this only breeds shame because it feeds into the three ingredients that are necessary for shame to survive: secrecy, silence, and judgment.[22] In fact, research has found that when survivors of rape cover up and hide what happened to them, it can cause more harm to them than the actual event.[23]

Survivors of trauma often feel this way even if no reasonable outsider would ever blame them for their struggles. Why? Because they incorrectly assume that other forms of trauma are more "legitimate" than theirs. For example, women who are sexually assaulted often say that their experience doesn't count as trauma unless they were raped. Clients who were emotionally or physically abused by their family often downplay the experience because their abuser was someone they knew and loved. Similarly, individuals who witness violence tend to think they shouldn't be affected because they weren't a direct victim of it. However, the reality is that trauma comes in every shape and size, and regardless of "how much" or "how little" suffering a client believes they went through, there is no hierarchy of suffering. All trauma is a source of pain.

I use an umbrella metaphor to describe the connection between shame, addiction, and trauma. If trauma is the hail that rains down on us, we use an umbrella to protect ourselves from feeling the pain of it. The umbrella includes all the maladaptive coping skills that clients develop to handle the trauma. Though I am specifically talking about alcohol use, this can include any other coping mechanism that clients use to numb their pain, such as drug use, dieting, disordered eating, perfectionism, excessive exercising, shopping, addictive relationships, gambling, and busyness, to name a few. These behaviors represent what is above the surface on a client's iceberg from chapter 1. Since these behaviors are visible by others, they are often identified as the problem, when in reality, they are merely symptoms of the deeper issue, which is unprocessed trauma, shame, and pain. Therefore, to achieve healing, clients must be willing to work through their shame and face the pain underneath their umbrella.

Trauma

Mental Health Issues • Ableism

Sexual Abuse • Racism • Gaslighting

Death of Loved Ones • Social Isolation • Bullying

Emotional Neglect • Sexism • Poverty • Parentification

Abandonment • Divorce • Job Loss • Miscarriages • Heterosexism

Divorce • Medical Trauma • Harassment • Injury • Chronic Illness

Scapegoating • Insomnia • Discrimination • Ageism • Weight Stigma

Violence • Sexual Assault • Invalidation • Infertility • Physical Abuse

Gambling • Dieting

Shopping • Drug Use

Alcohol Use • Disordered Eating

Excessive Exercise • Perfectionism

Relationships & Sex • Workaholism & Busyness

Pain   Shame

Adapted from *Not Drinking Tonight* (p. 51), by Amanda E. White, 2022, Hachette Go. Copyright 2022 by Amanda E. White.

Why You Struggle with Shame

Since shame is not openly discussed in our society, it can be difficult to identify where your shame comes from. Many times, shame is a response to trauma that you have endured. Trauma comes in many forms and doesn't just include the obvious examples of abuse, violence, or war. It can also involve smaller or recurring events that lead you to feel powerless or like there is something wrong with you. Fill out this worksheet to start understanding why you may struggle with shame.

1. What is your first memory feeling shame? What happened? How did you feel? What was said (and who said it)?

_____

_____

_____

_____

2. The following checklist includes many reasons that people may struggle with shame. Look through the statements and check off any that you relate to.

   ☐ Your family stressed the importance of accomplishments, leading you to believe that productivity determines your worth.

   ☐ You were raised in a religion that relied on shame as a means of coercing you to behave in certain ways or conforming to certain principles.

   ☐ You were verbally, sexually, physically, or emotionally abused or neglected.

   ☐ Your family often criticized, judged, or compared you to others.

   ☐ You were bullied while growing up.

   ☐ Your family kept secrets and encouraged you to hide things from or lie to outsiders.

   ☐ You were raised in an environment where parental figures were overly concerned with appearance (either yours or theirs) or with the family's reputation.

   ☐ You have a marginalized identity and were taught through the media, society, and others that there was something wrong with you or your body.

3. What memories came up for you as you went through this checklist? How have these experiences contributed to the development of shame?

_____

_____

_____

_____

The Cycle of Self-Sabotage

While everyone will experience shame at some point in their lives, it is even more common among individuals with disordered drinking, as the effects of alcohol make it likely that they will put themselves in risky situations or do things they later regret. In these situations, clients can feel like it is their fault if they end up in a traumatic situation. This is exacerbated by the fact that morality is so intertwined with alcohol and drug use. Many individuals still think addiction is a choice, and they'll blame and shame their loved ones for engaging in risky behavior, thinking it will help them stop. When I worked at a rehab facility, the most common thing I had to teach parents and partners was to stop shaming their loved ones who were struggling with substance use. Parents truly believed if they shamed their kids enough, they would convince them to get sober. They were blown away when I told them their loved ones already thought the absolute worst about themselves. Berating them only added fuel to the fire and made them more likely to use drugs or drink to escape that pain.

Even when loved ones *are* able to stop, it is difficult for them to stop beating themselves up for the harm they have caused themselves and others. Clients may feel as though they "deserve it" and want to punish themselves, either by engaging in the exact behavior they were trying to stop (drinking) or by berating themselves. However, people can only sit in the pain of extreme shame and self-loathing for so long before the brain naturally seeks a break. With time, clients either act out or look for an escape to numb the pain, so they end up drinking more or engaging in other maladaptive coping behaviors. The irony of this, of course, is that this often leads them right back to the same behavior that led them to drink in the first place, creating a cycle of self-sabotage. For many, addiction is the escape they need and the punishment they feel they deserve.

Self-Sabotaging Behavior

Become overwhelmed and act out or self-numb with alcohol

Cycle of Shame

Feel shame and beat yourself up: "There's something wrong with me"

Adapted from *Not Drinking Tonight* (p. 55), by Amanda E. White, 2022, Hachette Go. Copyright 2022 by Amanda E. White.

Self-sabotaging behavior also shows up after a traumatic event as a way for the brain to reenact what happened and reprocess it. Since the hallmark of trauma is not having power and control over the situation, when clients reenact it, they often do so in a way that allows their brains to feel in control of the situation. For example, in Bruce Perry's research[24] with traumatized children, especially those in the foster care system, he noticed that children would often present themselves in a calm manner when they first arrived at a new foster home, but they would later self-sabotage by acting defiantly. According to Perry, they did this unconsciously to create predictability for themselves. They knew how to handle chaos, so rather than allowing *someone else* to abandon them, they acted defiantly as a way to provoke (and be in control of) the abandonment themselves.

Adults do the same thing. They break up with someone because they're afraid their partner will leave them later. They don't prepare for a job interview because they assume they'll be rejected anyway. They start an argument with someone to avoid telling the other person how they feel. They beat themselves up and stay stuck in the cycle of self-sabotage because when life is constantly knocking you down, it sometimes feels better to be doing the knocking to yourself. As painful as that may be, at least clients know they are in control of it. It feels safer and is more predictable. As Virginia Satire famously stated, "Most people prefer the certainty of misery to the misery of uncertainty." Therefore, if clients are looking to break free from their self-sabotaging behavior, they must be willing to work through shame. Shame is the glue that holds self-sabotage in place.

Cycle of Shame

Self-sabotage is something that many individuals with substance use issues struggle with. When someone relapses or does something they regret after using substances, the most common reaction is for them to belittle themselves. They believe this will somehow prevent them from making the same mistake again. However, this approach almost always backfires, which creates a cycle of self-sabotage. Answer the questions below to discover how and if you are stuck in a cycle of self-sabotage with alcohol or any other addictive behavior.

1. What do you say to yourself when you drink too much or engage in an unhealthy or addictive pattern? If you have relapsed before or broken a promise to yourself to "never do _____ again," what does your internal dialogue sound like? For example: "I hate myself! What is wrong with me?" or "I am pathetic. I should just give up." Write down what you say to yourself when this happens.

_____

_____

_____

_____

2. What emotions do you feel when you beat yourself up (e.g., shame, sadness, anger, disgust, fear)?

_____

_____

_____

_____

3. When you feel that way, how do you typically react? Do you isolate from loved ones? Feel too overwhelmed to make any changes? End up drinking more? How do you respond to shame or self-criticism?

_____

_____

_____

_____

4. How does shame impact your life? For example, does it make it difficult to be honest? Does it make it difficult to admit your mistakes or have tough conversations? Does it make you want to give up on trying to change?

_____

_____

_____

_____

5. How is shame connected to your drinking or addictive patterns of behavior? Do you see how shame keeps you stuck in the cycle?

_____

_____

_____

_____

Working Through Shame

In order to work through shame, clients cannot resist what they are feeling. It is impossible for them to outrun or avoid the feelings of shame. Rather, the first step in working through shame is developing awareness of how shame feels in the body. For many clients, shame can manifest as a feeling in the pit of their stomach, an inability to breathe deeply, flushed skin, or nausea. They may also describe wanting to curl up in a ball, retreat to their bed for the rest of the day, quit their job and move to an island, or never put themselves out there again. Although shame may feel painful, it is an emotion just like any other, so it's important for clients to allow themselves to feel it. If they can accurately put a name to how they are feeling, it can feel less overwhelming.

The second step is to help clients identify what triggers their shame. You'll find that most clients have general patterns of things they feel shame about. This may include things they have done in the past, unrealistic expectations they hold themselves to, or beliefs they have about who they should be. For example, a client who used to be unreliable during their addiction may now be hypersensitive whenever they are late, have to change plans, or need to ask for more time to complete a work project. If they get sick and need to reschedule a therapy session, this may cause them to descend into a full-on shame spiral. Other clients who are in recovery may feel significant shame about lying since they were often deceitful while drinking. As a result, any insinuation that they are not being truthful can cause them to get angry and defensive.

Shame can also be triggered when clients receive messages from others telling them they need to look or act a certain way. For example, many clients who struggle with alcohol use often felt different from their families or peers when growing up. They may have been treated as the "black sheep" of the family or been told by peers that they were "weird." As adults, this internalized shame may lead them to believe there is no point in trying to form connections with others. Other clients may have received messages in childhood that equated their worth with their academic success or their performance in extracurricular activities, leading them to internalize the belief that their worth comes solely from their productivity. This can set them up for failure, especially when they believe they must always be the best. In all these cases, it can be helpful to reality-check these messages by having clients ask, "Where did these messages come from?" and "Do I truly believe this or is this an inherited belief?"

The third step is to create connection. So often, people who feel shame will isolate and withdraw from others, but this only makes matters worse because shame thrives in secrecy. It reinforces the belief that clients are unworthy of love and belonging, so staying connected to others during this process is critical. Encourage clients to share their shame with a trusted person in their lives. However, it is important to help clients identify the right people to share with. The ideal person will be supportive of the client's recovery process but will also not react negatively if the client confesses to slipping up. While many clients find it helpful to connect with someone who is sober themselves, this is not a necessity. Encourage the client to make a list of safe people they can call or text if they are having a craving, feeling ashamed about a mistake they made, or falling back into old patterns. They can simply say, "Hey, can I chat with you about something I am struggling with? I would love support instead of advice."

The final step of working through shame is to help clients take actions that are in accordance with their values. Clients may not be able to undo the behaviors of their past or make everyone like them, but they can live a life based on what they care about and value. If clients have acted in ways they later regret when under the influence of alcohol, one of the best things they can do is take a break from drinking or quit altogether so they can feel confident that they won't make the same mistakes again.

Unpack Your History of Shame

It is helpful to unpack your history of shame so you can understand how it manifests in your life. This involves learning how shame feels in your body, identifying your common triggers, and recognizing how you tend to react when you feel shame. Once you can understand your shame patterns, you'll be better able to take care of yourself.

1. How does shame show up in your body? How does it feel? For example, some people describe shame as a pit in their stomach, a tightening in their chest, nausea, feeling hot or flushed, or feeling like there is a huge weight on their shoulders.

   _____

   _____

   _____

   _____

   _____

2. What commonly triggers you to feel shame? For example, do you feel shame when you are late to work, don't meet someone's expectations, or make a mistake? What about when you break a commitment or think about how you behaved the last time you got drunk? Write down your common shame triggers below.

   _____

   _____

   _____

   _____

   _____

3. When people experience shame, they often react in one of three ways: (1) They beat themselves up and try to disappear; (2) They become overly agreeable and try to please others; or (3) They become angry and defensive, leading them to attack others. Which of these three behaviors do you relate to? How do you feel after engaging in these behaviors?

_____

_____

_____

_____

_____

4. Instead of isolating from others, people-pleasing, or becoming defensive in response to shame, see what it's like to seek out connection in these difficult moments. Could you call a friend and ask them for support? Could you send your boss an email and take responsibility when you make a mistake at work? Could you be vulnerable with your partner and share how you feel rather than getting defensive in a disagreement with them? Make a list of people you can reach out to.

_____

_____

_____

_____

_____

Identify and Live Your Values

Values allow you to identify what matters most to you. They are like a compass that can guide you toward living a fulfilling and intentional life. Answer the following questions to help you identify your values. Know that values can change, so don't feel like you are stuck with these values after doing this worksheet.

1. When you think of the most joyful days of your life, what were you doing? Who were you with?

_____

_____

_____

_____

2. Are there any aspects of your personality that you are proudest of or want to cultivate further? What are your biggest accomplishments?

_____

_____

_____

_____

3. At the end of your life, how do you want to look back on it? What do you want people to say about you? How do you want to have spent your time?

_____

_____

_____

_____

4. Who are a few people you look up to? What qualities do they have that you admire? What do you think their values may be?

_____

_____

_____

5. What are your biggest regrets? What do you wish you had done more of? Less of?

_____

_____

_____

6. After answering the previous set of questions, look through the list of values here and circle any that you feel connected to:

Abundance	Diversity	Honesty	Popularity
Advancement	Effectiveness	Humor	Power
Adventure	Endurance	Innovation	Professionalism
Affection	Enjoyment	Integrity	Prosperity
Appreciation	Excellence	Intelligence	Punctuality
Balance	Excitement	Invention	Reciprocity
Beauty	Faith	Involvement	Reliability
Career	Fame	Joy	Resilience
Caring	Family	Justice	Respect
Change	Finesse	Kindness	Security
Clarity	Fitness	Knowledge	Self-respect

Commonality	Forgiveness	Leadership	Spiritualism
Communication	Freedom	Learning	Stability
Compassion	Friendship	Love	Strength
Connection	Fun	Loyalty	Success
Contentment	Generosity	Openness	Teamwork
Contribution	Goodness	Order	Truth
Cooperation	Grace	Patience	Wealth
Courage	Gratitude	Peace	Wellness
Creativity	Harmony	Personal development	Wisdom

7. After circling the values that resonate with you, pick 10 that are most important to you and write them down here.

_____

_____

_____

_____

8. What are three actions you can take based on your values to combat shame? For example, if you value your relationship with your partner, carving out time each week for a date night is a values-based action you can take.

_____

_____

_____

_____

4

Emotion Regulation

Alcohol and emotions are inextricably connected. Alcohol is considered a crucial ingredient to mark almost every celebratory occasion in our lives: birthdays, promotions, holidays, and weddings—the list goes on. A regular Saturday night becomes a special occasion with the addition of alcohol. On the flip side, alcohol is also considered a go-to solution for dealing with stress, burnout, or any painful emotion. Alcohol is the sidekick of almost every television character going through a breakup or stressful time. These media portrayals of alcohol amplify the message that difficult emotions are intolerable and that the only way to cope with them is to turn to alcohol.

Therefore, if you want to help clients cut back on drinking or take a break from alcohol, an essential component of treatment involves teaching them how to understand and regulate their emotions. Otherwise, it's likely they will fall into old patterns of using alcohol to soothe stress, social anxiety, sadness, or anything in between. Many clients may not even recognize that they do this. They simply experience a life stressor and—boom!—they're pouring another glass of wine. By teaching clients the necessary emotion regulation skills, you empower them to process uncomfortable feelings, get their needs met, and make decisions out of choice, rather than as a reaction to their emotions.

A good starting point when introducing emotion regulation skills is to take inventory of what clients were taught about emotions over the years. What you'll find is that most clients did not get a proper education about emotions. It isn't something they were taught in health class, and unless the adults in their lives were versed on emotion regulation—or clients went to therapy or read a book on the topic—they likely received skewed messages about how to handle their feelings. Many of these messages had their origins in the client's family while growing up. For example, a client may have witnessed their father scolding their mother for being "dramatic" when she cried. Or a client may have been exposed to certain messaging around emotions, like "Boys shouldn't cry" or "You should feel grateful. Why are you upset about this?"

Other times, clients may have received messages that were more implicit. For example, if a caregiver expressed disapproval or discomfort when the client exhibited certain emotions, the client likely learned that these emotions were unacceptable. If the client's family ignored them when they said they felt scared or upset, they learned that their feelings weren't valid. This implicit learning can have a huge impact on clients because they start learning about emotions before they fully understand or even verbalize what is going on. As clients grow older, these messages get further reinforced through the interactions they have with same-aged peers. They may get teased for crying or witness one of their peers pushing another kid on the playground because they don't get their way. In turn, clients also see how adults and teachers discipline, dismiss, or support children in these scenarios.

Emotions Inventory

In order to better understand your emotional experience, it can be helpful to think about the messages you received about emotions while growing up, as well as who taught you these messages. Answer the questions below to discover what beliefs were imparted to you as a child and which of these beliefs you have internalized.

1. What messages did you receive about emotions when you were growing up? For example, were you ever told that your emotions were "too much" or that expressing feelings was "weak"?

   _____

   _____

   _____

   _____

   _____

2. Who was the source of these messages? Your family? Friends? Peers? Teachers? How did they express these messages to you?

   _____

   _____

   _____

   _____

   _____

3. How did these messages influence how you thought about your emotions growing up? For example, did you internalize the belief that certain emotions were unacceptable? That you needed to suppress or push away certain emotions?

_____

_____

_____

_____

_____

4. Have your thoughts about emotions changed as you have gotten older? In what ways? What are your current beliefs about your emotions or how you are supposed to express them? Are there certain emotions you are more comfortable expressing than others? Which ones?

_____

_____

_____

_____

_____

5. How do you currently respond when you experience difficult or uncomfortable emotions? Do you have any routines or habits that you resort to when you are stressed or emotional?

_____

_____

_____

_____

_____

How to Process Emotions

While the concept of "feeling all the feels" has become a popular pop psychology trend, most clients do not know how to process their emotions because they simply haven't been given the right tools to do so. For example, clients who are new to learning about their emotions may believe that to process them, they must halt whatever they are doing and feel all their feelings 24/7, even if it is in the middle of a work meeting or important event. I have also seen clients who believe that processing their emotions means they must talk through *everything* they feel with another person. They don't know that they can process their emotions alone and even in nonverbal ways. Other clients believe they are processing their emotions, when the truth is they are simply judging themselves for how they feel. Therefore, I decided to create the acronym NAILER to help clients process their emotions in a step-by-step manner:

Notice
Allow
Investigate
Label
Explore
Release

Clients start by **n**oticing the physical sensations they feel in their body and **a**llow these feelings to come up rather than resisting them. Then they **i**nvestigate what is going on by getting curious about what emotion they feel and putting a **l**abel on it. Finally, they **e**xplore what they can take to work through that emotion and take action to **r**elease it. By using these six steps, clients can get into the habit of processing and tending to their emotions as they come up so they can more effectively take care of themselves. Let's break down each of these steps in more detail.

Notice

To help clients process their emotions, the first step involves teaching them to tune into and notice their internal experience. That's because emotions start in our bodies as a physiological sensation. For example, when we are confronted with something that we are afraid of, our heart begins to race, our muscles tense up, and our breath quickens. These physiological sensations serve as a signal to us that we are experiencing fear. However, if clients are not in the habit of practicing mindfulness, they are likely not in tune with how they are feeling emotionally or physically, making it easy to miss these first emotional cues. If they want to get better at noticing their emotions, it is important for them to start incorporating mindfulness into their daily routine. There are a variety of quick and simple ways to do this. Here are some ideas to get them started.

Ways to Practice Mindfulness

- While taking a bath or shower, encourage clients to smell their soap, notice the temperature of the water, feel the texture of their loofah, and give their scalp a massage as they shampoo their hair.

- While eating, invite clients to slow down and notice the texture and taste of their food. They should chew slowly and notice how the texture of the food changes as it starts to break down. They can also notice how the feeling of fullness in their stomach changes as they eat.

- While clients brush their teeth, have them take the time to notice the taste of the toothpaste against their tongue, feel the foam in their mouth, and notice the texture of the bristles scrubbing against their teeth.

- When clients are doing any household chore—such as washing dishes, vacuuming, mopping, or making the bed—see if they can notice all the physical sensations involved. For example, if they are washing dishes, they might notice the smell of the soap, the feeling and temperature of the water on their skin, or how hard they have to scrub to get the plate clean.

- Walk clients through a body scan exercise (see the "Notice the Sensations in Your Body" exercise in this chapter).

- Encourage clients to practice yoga or another form of movement where they can slow down and notice the sensations in their body without distraction.

- Have clients go on a mindful walk or hike. Encourage them to notice the sounds of different creatures, the sight and smell of their surroundings, the feeling of the air on their skin, and how their body feels while moving.

- Meditate using an app or a guided meditation script. Some of my favorite apps are Headspace, Calm, Insight Timer, Buddhify, and Unplug.

It's helpful to remind clients that these mindfulness exercises are not meant to make them feel any emotions that they were not already experiencing. When they become aware of their bodily sensations, not all information is relevant to their emotional state. For example, they may feel achy in their neck because they slept on it the wrong way, or they might feel hungry because they haven't eaten breakfast. The point of practicing mindfulness is to improve their sense of interoception—to get them familiar with and more skilled at noticing all the input and sensations in their body—so they can more accurately understand their emotions. The more skilled they become, the more they can recognize how their emotions feel in their body. For example, some clients may come to realize that they experience anxiety as chest tightness, while others may be prone to stomachaches.

This is not to say that emotions will always feel exactly the same way. However, most of us do fall into typical patterns of how we experience our emotions. For example, in addition to chest tightness and stomach upset, anxiety is often associated with a constricted throat or difficulty taking a deep breath. In contrast, anger often manifests as hot limbs, a feeling of pulsing or throbbing blood, increased heart rate, and flushing. Sadness is often associated with a feeling of numbness, heavy limbs, and tingling eyes (reflecting the urge to cry). Joy is often described as a feeling of lightness in the limbs, as well as a tingling or buzzing sensation. When clients learn how certain emotions commonly feel on a physiological level, they can more easily start to identify emotions within themselves.

How Do Emotions Feel in Your Body?

While not everyone experiences emotions in the same way, we often have common patterns that reflect how emotions show up in our bodies. The following prompts will help you identify how four different emotions feel in your body.

1. Think of a situation that makes you angry. It could be a current situation in your life or a memory. Write it down in as much detail as possible, describing as many sensory aspects of the experience as you can (e.g., what you remember seeing, hearing, touching, tasting, smelling).

   _____

   _____

   _____

   _____

2. How does anger feel in your body?

   _____

   _____

   _____

   _____

3. Think of a situation that makes you sad. It could be a current situation or a specific memory. Write it down in as much detail as possible, describing as many sensory aspects of the experience as you can (e.g., what you remember seeing, hearing, touching, tasting, smelling).

   _____

   _____

   _____

   _____

4. How does sadness feel in your body?

_____

_____

_____

_____

_____

5. Think of a situation that makes you anxious, nervous, or fearful. It could be a current situation or a specific memory. Write it down in as much detail as possible, describing as many sensory aspects of the experience as you can (e.g., what you remember seeing, hearing, touching, tasting, smelling).

_____

_____

_____

_____

_____

6. How does anxiety or fear feel in your body?

_____

_____

_____

_____

7. Think of a situation that brings you joy. It could be a current situation or a specific memory. Write it down in as much detail as possible, describing as many sensory aspects of the experience as you can (e.g., what you remember seeing, hearing, touching, tasting, smelling).

_____

_____

_____

_____

_____

8. How does joy feel in your body?

_____

_____

_____

_____

Notice the Sensations in Your Body

To start noticing how emotions feel in your body, you must slow down and get mindful of what is going on in your body. One of the best ways to do this is to start with a body scanning exercise.

To begin, start by bringing your attention to the top of your head. Notice any sensations that are present in your scalp. Is there any tightness or itchiness there? What about your forehead, is there any tension there? Now start slowly shifting your attention downward to your eyes. Notice whether they are heavy, itchy, or stinging. Continue moving farther down your face and see what you notice about your cheeks. Are they feeling flushed or hot at all? How about your jaw? Is it tight or relaxed? Wiggle it around for a moment and notice how that feels.

Now move your attention down to your throat and see if you can notice any sensations that are present for you here. Is it feeling tight at all? How does it feel when you take a deep breath? What about your shoulders—are they tight? Are they strained and up around your ears? Notice whether there is any neck or shoulder pain present for you. Then shift your attention again, bringing your awareness to the sensations in your arms and hands. Are they feeling heavy and limp? Are your hands clammy?

Then bring your attention to the sensations in your chest. Take in several breaths and notice if anything changes when you breathe. Is your breathing slow, fast, or normal? Is your heart rate feeling elevated at all? What about your stomach? Can you notice any sensations of hunger, fullness, or satiety? Do you feel any pain or nausea? Finally, move your attention down to your legs and feet. Do your legs feel restless? Are you toes relaxed or curled?

Finally, do a scan of your overall body and see if you notice any areas of soreness or achiness. Sometimes taking small movements or wiggles during this process can help you notice any sensations that you were not initially aware of. You can also do some jumping jacks to get your heart rate up and then take a break to notice how it feels to calm back down.

Once you're finished with the body scan, reflect on the experience here and note any judgments or thoughts that came up for you.

_____

_____

_____

Allow

For many clients, one of the most common barriers to processing their emotions is their desire to avoid discomfort. The sensations may be uncomfortable, messy, and awkward. They don't know when it will end or trust that it will. In turn, they ignore or numb their emotions by drinking or doing something else that takes them away from the experience. Many clients do not even realize they are doing this. This is especially the case for clients who identify as "not being very emotional," who are often in the habit of distracting themselves before they have a moment to notice how they feel. To be clear, there's nothing wrong with distraction. It serves a very useful purpose. People cannot always stop in the middle of a meeting and work through their feelings. There are also times when emotions can get too overwhelming, in which case it may be wise for someone to take a break and distract themselves until they feel more regulated.

However, when clients chronically avoid or distract themselves from their emotions, it negatively impacts their mental health. It traps them in a vicious cycle where they use alcohol to numb their emotions, which leads them to experience an inevitable emotional outburst when they can't contain their feelings any longer. This reinforces their belief that uncomfortable emotions are to be feared, which starts the cycle all over again. In order to free themselves from this cycle, clients must allow themselves to feel any emotions that arise, even the uncomfortable ones.

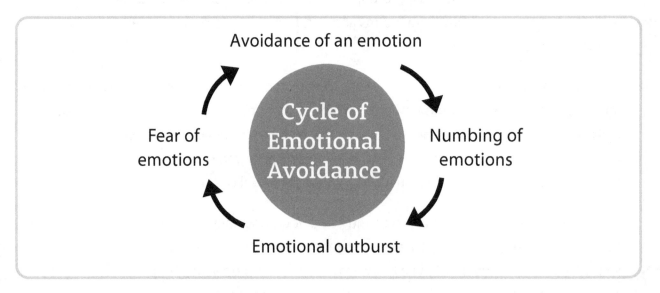

Breaking the cycle also requires that clients stop judging themselves for whatever they are feeling. So often, clients will avoid processing their emotions because they believe that they shouldn't be feeling a certain way. For example, a client might start experiencing bodily sensations connected with sadness and immediately think, *What's wrong with me? I shouldn't be feeling sad right now. Other people have it way worse than me. I'm so pathetic.* This causes them to experience meta-emotions, which are emotions *about* their emotions. For example, someone might feel angry about being sad or ashamed about feeling angry. People can have any combination of emotions and feel more than one emotion at the same time.

For clients with disordered drinking, the concept of meta-emotions is especially important because many believe it is not acceptable to experience certain emotions, particularly those that are uncomfortable or painful, such as sadness, guilt, and anger. As a result, whenever they notice themselves having those emotions, they feel shame (a meta-emotion), which is a huge trigger for alcohol use. Without an appropriate understanding of meta-emotions, clients are unable to realize that it is not their initial emotion that is causing them to drink; it is a meta-emotion, most often shame, that is usually triggering them.

Emotions	Meta-Emotions
A biological state brought on by neuropsychological changes associated with thoughts, mood, and a degree of pleasure or displeasure	An emotion you have *about* your emotions that prevents you from working through how you actually feel, or a judgment about your emotions that evokes an emotional response
Example: sadness	Example: being angry about feeling sad

Adapted from *Not Drinking Tonight* (p. 109), by Amanda E. White, 2022, Hachette Go. Copyright 2022 by Amanda E. White.

If a client has chronically avoided their emotions, it may be uncomfortable and overwhelming to allow themselves to experience their feelings. A helpful way to start is to have them practice in very short increments. You can even start by practicing in session. Whenever a client presents with sadness, anger, or any other uncomfortable emotion, lead them in noticing how they are feeling in their body, then set a timer and have them practice riding the wave of discomfort for 30 or 60 seconds. As they sit with the emotion, encourage them to relax their body, as clients often resist the physical sensations associated with emotions by tightening and tensing their muscles. Remind them that these sensations are temporary and cannot physically hurt them.

In addition, clients can repeat a mantra to themselves, such as "This will pass" or "This is temporary." They also do not have to sit still while they allow themselves to get into their feelings. They can walk, stretch, wiggle, make noise, or do whatever feels helpful as they ride the emotional wave. Have clients gradually increase the time they can allow themselves to feel this emotion, with the goal of working up to 15 to 20 minutes, which is typically how long an intense urge or sensation lasts.

Investigate

Context matters, especially when it comes to understanding our emotions. While emotions start in the body with physiological body changes, they become more specific and complex when we add in the context of life and social norms. Therefore, when clients can learn to pinpoint what happened *right before* they began feeling these physical changes, it gives them important clues in understanding what emotion they might be feeling and how they can take action to work through it. In contrast, when clients are not aware of the variables that may be influencing their mood, it is much more difficult for them to make constructive changes in their lives. This makes it more likely that they will continue to turn to alcohol or other destructive patterns of behavior instead of examining what triggered them to feel these uncomfortable emotions in the first place.

The following are some questions that clients can consider as they investigate their emotional experience, as well questions they should avoid.

Questions to Ask

- Why might I be feeling this way?

- Why now?

- What just happened? What may be triggering this emotion?

- What was I doing before this happened? Or this morning or last night?

- Do I have memories connected to this experience, person, or situation?

- Have I met my basic needs? Am I hungry, thirsty, lonely, or tired? Have I been outside today?

Questions to Avoid

- What is wrong with me?

- Why do I always feel this way?

- Why can't I make this feeling go away?

- Why can't I figure this out?

- Why can't I just be happy?

Questions like "Why might I be feeling this way?" can help clients make sense of their physiological sensations and the emotional experience that follows. When clients can recognize *why* they may be feeling a certain way, it can help them get their needs met in a way that does not involve picking up a drink. For example, a client who is feeling lonely might realize that they need to reach out to a loved one or schedule a coffee date with a friend instead of drinking. Another client who feels angry might realize that they would benefit from working out or going for a walk to let off some steam instead of stuffing down those emotions with a drink.

In contrast, questions like "What is wrong with me?" lead clients to feel shame and guilt, both of which are laden with judgment. These questions interfere with clients' ability to process their emotions and instead lead them to a place of overthinking, which can then lead them into the painful cycle of emotional avoidance I described earlier. Instead, it is important for clients to treat themselves with compassion as they investigate their emotional experience. I use the word *investigate* because the goal is for them to act like a scientist and lean into curiosity instead of judgment.

Processing Your Emotions

- Starts with curiosity about what you're feeling

- Involves noticing the sensations you feel in your body

- Involves offering yourself compassion and understanding

Overthinking Your Emotions

- Starts with judgment about your emotions

- Happens when you beat yourself up for feeling the way you do

- Includes repetitive thoughts

- Leads you to avoid your feelings by numbing or acting out

Label

The goal of helping your clients investigate their emotions is to support them in being able to accurately label how they feel. If clients are struggling to label their emotions, it's helpful to use a mood meter, which encourages them to first identify if they are high or low in *energy* and then if they are high or low in *pleasantness*.[25] These two spectrums are hardwired into our brain and, unlike emotions, are discernible even by infants. For example, babies may not understand the concept of hunger or boredom, but they do know and communicate their energy level and pleasantness.[26] Similarly, when clients can pinpoint how they are feeling on these two dimensions, it makes labeling their emotions easier. For example, if they feel slightly high in energy and low in pleasantness, they might be feeling peeved or annoyed. Or if they feel slightly low in both energy and pleasantness, they might be feeling bored or apathetic.

Mood Meter
How are you feeling?

Energy →

Enraged	Panicked	Stressed	Jittery	Shocked	Surprised	Upbeat	Festive	Exhilarated	Ecstatic
Livid	Furious	Frustrated	Tense	Stunned	Hyper	Cheerful	Motivated	Inspired	Elated
Fuming	Frightened	Angry	Nervous	Restless	Energized	Lively	Enthusiastic	Optimistic	Excited
Anxious	Apprehensive	Worried	Irritated	Annoyed	Pleased	Happy	Focused	Proud	Thrilled
Repulsed	Troubled	Concerned	Uneasy	Peeved	Pleasant	Joyful	Hopeful	Playful	Blissful
Disgusted	Glum	Disappointed	Down	Apathetic	At Ease	Easygoing	Content	Loving	Fulfilled
Pessimistic	Morose	Discouraged	Sad	Bored	Calm	Secure	Satisfied	Grateful	Touched
Alienated	Miserable	Lonely	Disheartened	Tired	Relaxed	Chill	Restful	Blessed	Balanced
Despondent	Depressed	Sullen	Exhausted	Fatigued	Mellow	Thoughtful	Peaceful	Comfy	Carefree
Despair	Hopeless	Desolate	Spent	Drained	Sleepy	Complacent	Tranquil	Cozy	Serene

← Pleasantness →

It may seem unimportant to find the *exact* word that describes how clients are feeling, but research has shown that the greater someone's emotional vocabulary—or emotional granularity[27]—the better they can regulate their emotions. Children in general have a much smaller emotional vocabulary than adults, which is part of the reason why they tend to feel emotions more intensely and unpredictably. Most children only have three words to describe how they feel: happy, sad, and mad. If those are the only three words that can describe their possible feelings, then they are going to feel one of those emotions about one-third of the time. However, once a child starts recognizing the difference between frustration and anger, for example, this will reduce the intensity of the experience and allow them to better process and regulate their emotions. Therefore, accuracy and specificity matter.

In addition, words play an important role in shaping our experience of ourselves, our bodily sensations, and the external stimuli around us. Have you ever heard that the Inuit and Yupik have dozens of words for snow?[28] Snow is such an important part of their lives that having many different words to precisely describe the exact kind of snow matters. While we may just see regular snow, the Inuit and Yupik have different words to communicate the differences between "fresh snow," "fine snow," and "soft deep snow." Similarly, other languages have different words for emotions. Learning new words for emotions is another great way to expand your clients' emotional vocabulary.

Examples of Emotion Words in Other Languages

- **Schadenfreude** (German): taking delight in the troubles or failure of another

- **Sehnsucht** (German): an intense desire for alternative states and realizations of life, even if they are unattainable

- **Kilig** (Tagalog): the feeling of exhilaration when you talk to someone you like romantically

- **Gigil** (Tagalog): the irresistible urge to pinch or squeeze someone because they are cute

- **Iktsuarpok** (Inuit): the anticipation of waiting for someone, where you keep checking to see if they've arrived

- **Feierabend** (German): a festive mood at the end of a working day

- **Kvell** (Yiddish): feeling pride and joy in someone else's accomplishment

- **Uitwaaien** (Dutch): refreshing yourself by taking a walk in the wind

- **Aware** (Japanese): the bittersweetness of a brief, fading moment of transcendent beauty

Explore and Release

The final two steps in NAILER involve helping clients explore how they can release themselves from whatever emotion they are experiencing. To explore, they must ask themselves, *What can I do to take care of myself right now? What do I need right now?* To release, they must take action to regulate their body and bring themselves back to a place of homeostasis. Most of us have the experience of feeling better after venting to a friend, going for a run, or screaming along to a song in our car because this allowed us to discharge some of the energy associated with an emotion. Remember that the human body and brain are inextricably connected. When a client experiences an uncomfortable emotion in response to some life stressor, the body responds by releasing a cascade of hormones into the bloodstream to initiate the fight-flight-freeze response. Therefore, the simple act of labeling an emotion won't make all those physiological body changes and hormones go away. Clients need to do something to release that energy.

There are a few major ways they can discharge energy: movement, mindfulness, connection, and self-expression. Certain actions may feel better depending on how clients feel. For example, if someone is angry, they may feel much better after moving their body or punching a pillow to release that pent-up energy. But if they feel sad, they may feel better after cuddling with a loved one.

Once you review these six steps with your client, they can benefit from the following worksheet, which walks them through the steps in chronological order. It may be helpful to work with them in session first so you can support them in learning how to tune into their experience, and then assign it as homework so they can use it to process any triggering experiences going forward.

How to Process an Emotion

Many of us hear that we should be "processing our emotions," but what does that actually mean? The following worksheet will walk you through the five steps involved in processing an emotion. The more you practice, the easier it will be to work through your emotions without having to use the prompts on this worksheet.

Step 1: Notice

The first step in working through an uncomfortable or painful emotion involves turning your awareness inward and noticing the physical sensations arising in your body. To do so, find a comfortable position where you can pause for a few minutes. Close your eyes if that feels comfortable. Take five deep breaths. Start scanning your body to notice how you are feeling right now. Don't worry about identifying any emotions. Just focus on what is happening in your body. After a few minutes, use the figure here to circle areas where you noticed any sensations. Include a description of the sensations too, being as specific as you can.

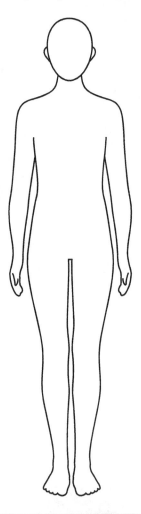

Step 2: Allow

The next step is to allow yourself to feel whatever it is that you are feeling. So often, when we experience uncomfortable emotions, we have the urge to push them away, distract ourselves, or numb ourselves from the feeling. We may also tell ourselves that we "shouldn't" be feeling this way, which can result in judgment and shame on top of what we are already experiencing. If you are not used to allowing yourself to feel certain emotions, you may feel scared or overwhelmed at the prospect of letting yourself feel them, but avoiding your emotions only makes them more intense over time.

What are some ways you've behaved in an attempt to numb, push away, or distract yourself from uncomfortable emotions? Which emotions most often elicit these behaviors?

_____

_____

_____

Think back to the bodily sensations you identified in the first step of this exercise. What urges do you have in response to these bodily sensations? For example, do you feel the urge to fidget? Are you thinking about everything you need to check off your to do list? Do you want to stop doing this exercise? Write down what urges you have below.

_____

_____

_____

Try to sit with this urge for a moment without acting on it. Imagine that the urge is simply a wave in the ocean and that you are riding it until it passes. What is this experience like for you?

_____

_____

_____

Once the urge passes, write down what you feel in this moment, allowing yourself to feel it without attempting to block it in any way.

_____

_____

_____

_____

Step 3: Investigate

Let's dig a little deeper to understand why you may be experiencing these bodily sensations. Maybe they arose because you're judging this exercise and don't think it's going to be helpful. Maybe they arose in response to an interaction you had with someone earlier in the day. Whatever the reason, practice coming from a place of curiosity. These questions will help you discover why you might be feeling this way.

What were you doing right before you experienced these bodily sensations? (Or this morning or last night?) How were you feeling before they occurred?

_____

_____

_____

_____

Is there anything notable going on in your life that may have impacted how you feel? Do you have any specific memories or thoughts connected to this experience, person, or situation?

_____

_____

_____

_____

Have you met your basic needs today? Are you hungry, thirsty, lonely, or tired? Have you been outside today? These are important questions because sometimes bodily sensations can be misconstrued as emotions if you haven't met your most basic needs.

_____

_____

_____

Step 4: Label

Based on the bodily sensations you identified and the investigative questions you filled out, what emotion are you feeling? If you are struggling to identify an emotion, use the following mood meter to help you out, which asks you to first identify if you are feeling high or low in *energy* and then high or low in *pleasantness*. This can help you find a word that fits your experience. If you feel like none of these words fit, find one that is the closest match and look up some synonyms. You can also feel more than one emotion word at the same time.

Mood Meter
How are you feeling?

Enraged	Panicked	Stressed	Jittery	Shocked	Surprised	Upbeat	Festive	Exhilarated	Ecstatic
Livid	Furious	Frustrated	Tense	Stunned	Hyper	Cheerful	Motivated	Inspired	Elated
Fuming	Frightened	Angry	Nervous	Restless	Energized	Lively	Enthusiastic	Optimistic	Excited
Anxious	Apprehensive	Worried	Irritated	Annoyed	Pleased	Happy	Focused	Proud	Thrilled
Repulsed	Troubled	Concerned	Uneasy	Peeved	Pleasant	Joyful	Hopeful	Playful	Blissful
Disgusted	Glum	Disappointed	Down	Apathetic	At Ease	Easygoing	Content	Loving	Fulfilled
Pessimistic	Morose	Discouraged	Sad	Bored	Calm	Secure	Satisfied	Grateful	Touched
Alienated	Miserable	Lonely	Disheartened	Tired	Relaxed	Chill	Restful	Blessed	Balanced
Despondent	Depressed	Sullen	Exhausted	Fatigued	Mellow	Thoughtful	Peaceful	Comfy	Carefree
Despair	Hopeless	Desolate	Spent	Drained	Sleepy	Complacent	Tranquil	Cozy	Serene

← Energy ↓ | ← Pleasantness →

What emotion word best describes how you feel right now? _____

On a scale of 1 to 10 (with 1 being *not at all intense* and 10 being *the most intense it could be*), how intense is the emotion in your body right now? _____

Are you experiencing any emotions *about* your emotions? For example, guilt about feeling angry? Frustration about feeling sad? Describe any secondary emotions, or meta-emotions, you feel here.

_____

_____

_____

Steps 5 and 6: Explore and Release

To work through whatever emotion you are experiencing, you need to explore ways that allow you to release the pent-up energy in your body that the emotion is creating. Otherwise, the emotion will continue to build up over time, just like steam in a pressure cooker. With enough steam, the pressure cooker will eventually explode. You can release your emotions through a variety of exercises that emphasize movement, connection with others, mindfulness, or self-expression. Put a check mark by any of the following activities that you'd like to try.

Movement

☐ Move in some way, whether it's yoga, stretching, walking, running, jumping jacks, shaking, dancing, yelling, or punching a pillow.

Mindfulness

☐ Do a deep breathing exercise. Try breathing in for a count of four, holding for a count of four, and then exhaling for a count of four.

☐ Slow down and mindfully observe your five senses while doing any routine activity, such as cleaning, organizing, cooking, or taking a shower or bath.

Connection with Others

☐ Spend time with close friends or family. Studies show that when you are especially close to someone, you can sync up heart rates and breathing patterns. When you're with loved ones, you're also more likely to engage in affection and touch—whether in the form of a kiss, a friendly pat on the back, or a platonic hug—and to laugh authentically, which does wonders for making you feel safe, heard, and understood.[29]

☐ Be around other people in general, whether this involves smiling when you see a stranger or engaging in small talk. This reassures your brain that it is okay to get out of your head and be present in the world around you.

☐ Cuddle or spend time with a pet.

Self-Expression

☐ Write in a journal or share your feelings with someone.

☐ Do something creative, such as painting, drawing, dancing, listening to music, singing, or playing an instrument.

☐ Cry. Scientists have recently discovered that we have different types of tears. Tears that we get when cutting an onion (basal tears) have a different composition than emotional tears (psychic tears), which have neurotransmitters that are released during times of stress.[30]

Now pick one of the activities that you identified from the list and spend the next 20 minutes engaging in the activity. When you're done, reflect on the experience. What was it like? How do you feel now?

_____

_____

_____

_____

5

Alcohol Isn't Self-Care

Contrary to popular belief, most real self-care isn't Instagram-able. It's not glamorous. It's not about "treating yourself," and most self-care is not something you can buy. Self-care is going to the dentist when you've been avoiding it, saying no to a trip you cannot afford, turning off your phone, or drinking a glass of water. It's not selfish, and people do not have to earn their right to practice self-care, just as they don't have to earn their right to go to sleep each night. Rest and self-care are necessary, and it is impossible for clients to be mentally well or to regulate their emotions if they aren't taking care of themselves.

However, for many clients, the concept of self-care is highly intertwined with alcohol. Marketers have latched onto the recent popularity of self-care and use it to sell almost every product imaginable, from bath bombs to alcohol. Women, and especially mothers, are sold the idea that alcohol is self-care, leading to the rise of what is known as "mommy wine culture." In 2019, the *New York Times* even published an article entitled "Natural Wine Is My Self-Care."[31] The problem is that alcohol is not self-care. Self-care is an activity you do to take care of yourself—to rest and recharge so you feel better in the future. Alcohol is the antithesis of this. While alcohol temporarily reduces anxiety and stress, it only increases it the next day. And being intoxicated or hungover makes it more difficult for clients to take care of their real needs. Therefore, if you want to help your clients build a sober life, you'll need to help them find ways to practice self-care that don't involve picking up a bottle of alcohol.

Self-Care Inventory

Before you identify ways to improve your self-care routine, it is important to understand your history with self-care. Fill out the questions below to examine the messages you received about self-care, how you currently engage in self-care, and what practices you have done in the past to take care of yourself.

1. What comes to mind when you think about self-care?

_____

_____

_____

_____

2. What current self-care practices do you engage in?

_____

_____

_____

_____

3. Are there any self-care practices you did in the past that you no longer do?

_____

_____

_____

_____

4. Are there any self-care practices that you would like to try?

_____

_____

_____

_____

5. How do you use alcohol as a means of self-care?

_____

_____

_____

_____

6. What forms of self-care do you neglect when you are drinking alcohol?

_____

_____

_____

_____

Hierarchy of Needs

When helping clients consider other avenues for self-care that don't involve alcohol, it is also important to acknowledge the role of privilege, which affects many individuals' ability to engage in self-care. The most important forms of self-care involve meeting our basic needs, but this is a barrier for many clients owing to disparities in access to housing, medical care, job opportunities, and more. Maslow's hierarchy of needs[32] helps us understand why it's difficult for someone to focus on creating satisfaction and fulfillment in their life if they are struggling to keep a roof over their head and food on the table. For the same reason, if someone does not have access to adequate food, clean drinking water, health care, or safe housing, it is going to be extremely difficult for them to engage in self-care.

In recent years, people have rightly critiqued Maslow's hierarchy, as it overly prioritizes the needs and wants of the self without considering the impact on the group or community at large. It also does not account for individual differences and suggests that psychological needs are less important than physiological needs. In response, Scott Barry Kaufman created a more nuanced and updated model of Maslow's work, which uses a diagram of a sailboat.[33] In this model, Kaufman states that three needs compose the bottom of the boat: safety, connection, and self-esteem. Unlike Maslow's model, these three needs are *not* organized in a hierarchy but work together to stabilize the base of the boat. Clients must feel stable and secure before they can feel comfortable growing, in the same way that a sailboat must have a firm and secure base before it can open its sail, move, and start exploring.

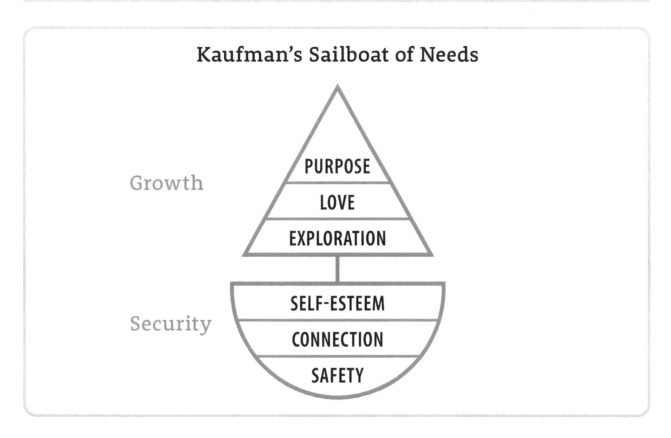

On the top of Kaufman's model is the sail, which is made up of exploration, love, and purpose. Together, these three needs provide people with the opportunity for growth and potentially transcendence. Exploration is a very important human need. Our brains are quite literally wired for it; we get a dopamine rush when we engage in new activities and experiences. This was how natural selection shaped us—especially compared to other animals—to become highly adaptable. Similarly, our brains are wired for love and connection. Not only do we get a similar dopamine rush from being around people we love and feel connected to, but love is an important need for procreation. Finally, humans have a need for purpose. This is believed to be a distinctly human need, where we feel compelled to make our lives have meaning or significance. However, when people are not physically or psychologically safe and secure, these growth needs are not going to be as important, or even as enticing. Survival always comes first. Therefore, Kaufman's metaphor also serves as a good reminder that individuals can always pause their growth when they need to slow down and get back in touch with their more basic needs.

In the following section, I lay out eight different types of self-care that include ways clients can meet their basic needs for stabilization and security. I also include ideas for growth and exploration. Depending on a client's current circumstances, you can determine which part of the sailboat they need to focus on first. Early in recovery, achieving security—that is, stabilizing the hull of the sailboat—is most important. However, the longer a client stays in recovery, the more growth they will need and desire. This may look like trying a new hobby, making new friends, dating, traveling, or even switching careers. As humans, we are never finished meeting our needs. We must tend to them all day every day. Therefore, clients will shift between growing (pushing for more) and contracting (pausing and integrating), depending on what is going on in their life, their mental and physical health, and their relationships.

Types of Self-Care

There are eight types of self-care: emotional, mental, physical, spiritual, social, professional, financial, and environmental. Some of these overlap with each other, but I find it helpful to break it down into these eight categories to give you an idea of how expansive real self-care can be. This doesn't mean that clients necessarily *need* to engage in every type of self-care listed here. Instead, help them focus on the areas that will best support them in meeting their needs. I find that most clients benefit from doing activities in at least one or two self-care areas.

Emotional

Emotional self-care involves noticing the emotions we are feeling in our bodies and acting in ways that honor and nurture those emotions. Since emotional health is intertwined with almost everything we do, a client's ability to care for their emotional health can impact their ability to meet all their basic needs. As with all of these categories, self-care will look different depending on the person, but here are some ways clients can enhance their emotional health:

- Take a break from social media

- Put their own needs first

- Repeat positive affirmations

- Say no and set boundaries

- Keep a daily journal

- Practice self-compassion when things don't go as planned

- Ask for help when they need it

- Schedule intentional "me" time each day

Mental

Mental self-care consists of doing things that support our mental health and state of mind. This can be as simple as journaling or going to therapy. However, it can also look like learning a new skill or challenging ourselves in some capacity. Here are some examples of activities clients can do to enhance their mental health:

- Read a self-explorative book

- Journal

- Go on a mindful walk

- Learn a new skill

- Host a craft night

- Rest or have quiet time

- Do a puzzle

- Cook or bake

- Paint, draw, sculpt, or engage in art in some capacity

- Go to the library

- Travel

- Explore a museum, new restaurant, or other attraction in their area

Physical

We practice physical self-care by listening to how our bodies feel and acting in ways that support us in feeling physically well. It also involves doing things that we may not enjoy but that are good for our health, such as going to the dentist or leaving a party to go to sleep earlier. The following activities can help clients get into the habit of physical self-care:

- Dance

- Eat a satisfying meal

- Exercise

- Drink water throughout the day

- Walk outside

- Get enough sleep

- Maintain a balanced diet

- Stretch

- Take a shower or bath

- Go to the doctor or dentist

- It *could* look like getting a pedicure or facial

Spiritual

Spiritual self-care involves taking actions that support a sense of sacredness in life. For some clients, this may be tied to religion, while for others it simply involves connecting with a higher sense of self. Regardless, all human beings have a need for meaning and understanding beyond themselves. Not only can it give people a sense of safety and security, but it can also support them in meeting their need for purpose. Here are some activities that promote spiritual self-care:

- Attend a religious gathering

- Join a spiritual community group

- Read spiritual texts or share ideas with others

- Practice yoga

- Meditate

- Take a nature walk

- Volunteer

- Practice tarot

- Engage in a meaningful hobby

Social

We engage in social self-care when we connect with other people. While everyone needs different amounts of alone time—and people have different schedules that affect who they spend time with—we all need connection. Here are some activities that clients can do to practice social self-care:

- Schedule a phone call with a long-distance friend

- Spend time with family or friends

- Go on a double date

- Take a walk with a friend

- Get to know their neighbors

- Join a book club or an interest group

- Go to a dog park

- Take their kids to a playground

- Join an online group that caters to their particular interests

- Unfollow people on social media who don't serve them anymore

Professional

Professional self-care entails doing things to support our career, vocation, or professional life. When clients are able to support themselves in a professional capacity, it also protects their mental health by ensuring they don't burn out at work and continue feeling fulfilled by their job. The following are suggestions that clients can use to practice professional self-care:

- Schedule stretching breaks at work

- Set boundaries with coworkers

- Eat a nourishing lunch away from their desk or workspace

- Use vacation days or sick leave when needed

- Leave work at work

- Attend professional development trainings

- Be punctual and leave on time

- Ask for help or clarification

- Share ideas with the team

Financial

We practice financial self-care when we do things to help us meet our financial goals and preserve our resources. Like all the other categories listed here, this type of self-care is unique to the individual. For some clients, financial self-care involves cutting back on spending. However, for other clients, especially those who struggle with allowing themselves to enjoy things, it can involve being less rigid with finances. Clients can practice financial self-care with any of these activities:

- Pay bills on time

- Create (and stick to!) a budget

- Eat meals at home

- Cancel automatic subscriptions

- Use public transit

- Check banking and credit card statements regularly

- Unsubscribe from emails that promote shopping and entice them with coupons

- Spend money on things that bring them joy or fill a need

- Meet with a financial planner

Environmental

Finally, environmental self-care is about taking care of the space in which we live or exist. Most people find that the space they spend time in can have an impact on how they feel. When they have physical reminders of the things that they are avoiding, such as putting away laundry or dishes, it can make them feel overwhelmed. Here are some ways clients can practice environmental self-care:

- Keep common spaces clutter-free

- Tidy up regularly

- Create a weekly cleaning schedule

- Donate old clothing

- Decorate their space in a way that feels nourishing

- Create a routine around chores

- Change their sheets

- Minimize waste by recycling

- Decorate their desk at work

Self-care looks different for everyone and changes depending on the situation and their stage of life. The concept of self-care looks very different for a young adult compared to someone who has children. It is also going to look different for someone who didn't sleep last night because they were up with a crying baby versus someone who just moved to a new city and is looking to make new friends. In the former case, sleep will likely be a priority, while in the latter, engaging in social activities will take precedence. As clients grow, change, and enter new stages of life, so will their self-care routine.

Eight Types of Self-Care

Self-care is a buzz worthy topic these days. Social media can make it seem as though everything is self-care, whether its buying new clothing or updating your house with the latest décor. But the truth is, self-care is highly personal and ever-changing. It changes depending on what is going on in your life. Self-care when you are single is going to look different from when you are in a relationship, just as it will look different if you have a child or are early in your recovery. The context matters. The goal is to discover what you need to implement into your daily life to support your well-being. Fill out the questions below to identify what self-care looks like for you and what you may be doing to counteract your well-being.

Emotional Self-Care: Listening and Tending to Your Emotions

1. How do you currently practice emotional self-care?

   _____

   _____

2. Put a check mark by any of the following behaviors that you engage in that counteract your emotional self-care:

   ☐ Drinking alcohol

   ☐ Engaging in another addictive or numbing pattern of behavior

☐ Avoiding, suppressing, or ignoring your emotions

☐ Beating yourself up when you make a mistake or feel an uncomfortable emotion

☐ Pretending you are not bothered by someone or something when you are

☐ Saying yes when you want to say no

☐ Not setting boundaries

3. What practices can you commit to doing to promote emotional self-care?

_____

_____

Mental Self-Care: Nourishing and Supporting Your Mental Health

1. How do you currently practice mental self-care?

_____

_____

2. Put a check mark by any of the following behaviors that you engage in that counteract your mental self-care:

☐ Drinking alcohol

☐ Engaging in another addictive or numbing pattern of behavior

☐ Avoiding pleasurable experiences because you feel like you don't deserve them

☐ Ignoring your need to travel, meet new people, or have new experiences

☐ Procrastinating

☐ Skipping therapy appointments

☐ Discontinuing psychotropic medication without consulting your prescriber

3. What practices can you commit to doing to promote mental self-care?

_____

_____

Physical Self-Care: Listening and Tending to Your Body and Physical Health

1. How do you currently practice physical self-care?

_____

_____

2. Put a check mark by any of the following behaviors that you engage in that counteract your physical self-care:

☐ Drinking alcohol

☐ Engaging in another addictive or numbing pattern of behavior

☐ Skipping meals

☐ Drinking too much caffeine throughout the day

☐ Getting fewer than seven hours of sleep

☐ Hitting the snooze button multiple times upon waking up

☐ Avoiding doctor or dentist appointments

☐ Ignoring hygiene by not brushing your teeth, combing your hair, etc.

3. What practices can you commit to doing to promote physical self-care?

_____

_____

Spiritual Self-Care: Nurturing Your Need for Religion, Meaning, or Mysticism

1. How do you currently practice spiritual self-care?

_____

_____

2. Put a check mark by any of the following behaviors that you engage in that counteract your spiritual self-care:

☐ Drinking alcohol

☐ Engaging in another addictive or numbing pattern of behavior

☐ Skipping religious services because you feel like you don't deserve to participate

☐ Giving up on volunteering or helping others because you believe you do not have anything to offer or cannot make a big enough difference

☐ Avoiding spending time in nature

☐ Giving up any spiritual practice that nourishes you

☐ Ignoring your values (e.g., if you value honesty, and lie or hide things while drinking, this is a way you are counteracting your spiritual self-care)

3. What practices can you commit to doing to promote spiritual self-care?

_____

_____

Social Self-Care: Cultivating Important Relationships and Creating a Support Network

1. How do you currently practice social self-care?

_____

_____

2. Put a check mark by any of the following behaviors that you engage in that counteract your social self-care:

☐ Getting into fights with loved ones or friends while intoxicated

☐ Isolating yourself from people you love

☐ Avoiding having honest conversations with loved ones or friends

☐ Not returning phone calls or texts

☐ Hate-following people on social media

☐ Spending time with people that make you feel unsafe or who are harmful

3. What practices can you commit to doing to promote social self-care?

_____

_____

Environmental Self-Care: Tending to Your Physical Space and Surroundings

1. How do you currently practice environmental self-care?

_____

_____

2. Put a check mark by any of the following behaviors that you engage in that counteract your environmental self-care:

☐ Keeping a messy or cluttered living space

☐ Decorating your space with alcohol-themed décor

☐ Hiding a secret stash of alcohol in your home

☐ Not cleaning up after yourself

☐ Allowing laundry to pile up on the floor

☐ Not bothering to unpack or make your living environment feel like a home

☐ Wearing or keeping clothes that you don't like or that don't fit

3. What practices can you commit to doing to promote environmental self-care?

_____

_____

Professional Self-Care: Fostering a Supportive Work Environment and Cultivating Vocational Goals

1. How do you currently practice professional self-care?

_____

_____

2. Put a check mark by any of the following behaviors that you engage in that counteract your professional self-care:

☐ Procrastinating on important projects or assignments

☐ Showing up to work late

☐ Showing up to work hungover

☐ Getting drunk at work events and losing control

☐ Not speaking up if you need support, help, or clarification

☐ Keeping poor work-life boundaries

3. What practices can you commit to doing to promote professional self-care?

_____

_____

Financial Self-Care: Nurturing and Protecting Your Economic Resources

1. How do you currently practice financial self-care?

_____

_____

2. Put a check mark by any of the following behaviors that you engage in that counteract your financial self-care:

☐ Spending money on alcohol or another addictive behavior (e.g., shopping, gambling)

☐ If you can afford to pay your bills, ignoring them and incurring late fees

☐ If you can afford to, neglecting to contribute to a 401k or retirement plan

☐ Ignoring your budget

☐ Buying things you cannot afford

☐ Not treating yourself to things you can afford

☐ Impulsively spending money

3. What practices can you commit to doing to promote financial self-care?

_____

_____

Over-Functioning and Under-Functioning

Sometimes in the process of selecting self-care activities, clients can struggle to identify what real self-care is for them. In these moments, encourage clients to ask themselves, "How will I feel *after* I do this and not during?" That's because many people don't actually enjoy the process of self-care—such as cleaning or going to the dentist—but they feel better after they complete the task. For example, if someone feels anxious about going on a first date, but they are committed to finding a relationship, they will likely feel proud after going on the date and putting themselves out there. Self-care is about taking care of our future self. At the same time, this does not necessarily mean that the future self needs to do more. For example, if someone pushes themself to exercise when they are drained and tired, they will feel worse a few hours later. Many times, taking a nap, skipping a workout, or setting a boundary is something our future self will thank us for.

To determine what self-care looks like for your clients, it is important to know if they have a tendency toward over-functioning (doing more than is necessary) or under-functioning (not doing enough). If clients lean toward over-functioning, their self-care will probably look a lot like slowing down, resting, and asking for help. In contrast, if they struggle with under-functioning, their self-care will involve making a commitment to take small actions, following through on tasks, and keeping small promises to themselves *even when they really don't feel like doing it.* In either case, alcohol is not self-care. While it may make clients feel better in the moment, it has far-reaching consequences in the long run.

Over-Functioning Looks Like...

- Needing to be in charge during a crisis, conflict, or project

- Struggling to delegate because an individual doesn't trust others to follow through or handle it as well as them

- Getting more amped up and taking action as a result of stress and anxiety

- Not being able to rest, sleep, or slow down

- Taking over other people's tasks or responsibilities

- Struggling to say no or cancel plans even when burned out or overextended

- Rescuing or taking care of others

Under-Functioning Looks Like...

- Getting overwhelmed, shutting down, and avoiding tasks, people, or responsibilities

- Being perceived as flaky or irresponsible

- Waiting for people to jump in and take control of the situation

- Being dependent on others for advice, reminders, plans, tasks, appointments, and so on

- Avoiding tasks and allowing things to pile up

- Wanting to zone out, numb, or ignore things to cope

The concept of over-functioning and under-functioning is also relevant when helping clients examine their relationship dynamics. Many clients with a history of problematic alcohol use are under-functioners whose behavior has been enabled by a partner or parent who is an over-functioner. This perpetuates the client's drinking problem because if they don't uphold their responsibilities, the other person will simply pick up the slack for them. This relational dynamic also prevents the client from fully recognizing how their substance use is negatively impacting their life. For example, a client may not realize how much money they are spending on alcohol because their parents keep giving them more. On the other hand, clients with substance use disorders can also be over-functioners. For some clients, alcohol may be the one thing that they use to blow off steam at the end of the day. Alcohol may also help them ignore their emotions or avoid having difficult conversations with their partners who under-function.

In either case, the client must break the cycle of over- and under-functioning in order to change their relationship with alcohol. In the case of a client who struggles with under-functioning, it is important for their over-functioning partner to step back and allow the client to take on more responsibility, even if the client doesn't complete tasks as well or in the same way. If an under-functioning client is deep in their addiction, they may need to focus on getting well before they are able to split chores and tasks more evenly, but they can start by taking smaller, more manageable first steps, allowing them to build healthy habits that compound over time. For example, an under-functioning client may commit to making their bed, showering, or spending five minutes outside each day. If they are unable to meet these goals, try to break the goal up into even smaller pieces so the client can successfully take at least one small action every day. These steps teach clients to take small actions even when they feel overwhelmed and, more importantly, support the client in building self-esteem as they learn how to follow through on these smaller commitments.

> **Quick Tip:** Have under-functioning clients time themselves whenever they are confronted with a task that they typically avoid. They can either set a timer for five minutes or put on their favorite song and see how much they can get done before time is up. They may be surprised by how much they can accomplish in such a short period of time! This trick can also help under-functioning clients realize that most tasks take much less time than they imagine in their head. For example, unloading the dishwasher takes most people around three or four minutes.

In contrast, for clients who struggle with over-functioning, one of the first things they will need to work on is taking breaks. Even if they feel like they don't "need" to, if they start proactively planning for breaks in their day, this will allow them to learn how to rest. This may involve teaching them how to delegate, ask for what they need, and set boundaries (more on that in the next chapter). Since many over-functioning clients feel as though nobody else can do their job as well as they can, it is also crucial to educate them on burnout. Whereas overworking themselves will lead to an inevitable cycle of crashing and burning out, taking time to rest will allow them to get more accomplished. Finally, over-functioners must learn that it is not their job to fix other people's problems and that not everything is a crisis that needs to be solved immediately. Instead of jumping to resolve the latest crisis of the day, they can work on stopping to think through their choices before responding, which will allow them to make better decisions over the long term and save energy.

How to Determine Whether Something Is Self-Care

True self-care does not always involve doing things that are fun or relaxing. While self-care can *sometimes* involve pampering yourself and taking time to decompress, other times it involves finally having a difficult conversation with a friend, making time to work out when you'd rather vegetate on the couch, or forcing yourself to do something outside of your comfort zone. The key to these types of self-care is that while you might feel uncomfortable while doing the task, you'll likely feel better once it's complete. To help you determine whether a particular activity counts as a form of self-care, answer the questions here. At the end of the day, though, only you can know for sure.

1. How do you feel right *now* as you think about doing the task? Pick any emotion words that capture how you feel.

   _____

   _____

   _____

2. How do you think you will feel *after* you finish this task? You can base this off past experience or use your imagination to take your best guess.

   _____

   _____

   _____

3. Do you have enough energy to do this right now? If not, is there something you can do first to give yourself more energy?

   _____

   _____

   _____

4. Will you have more or less energy after you finish the task? Is it worth the energy expenditure? Why or why not?

_____

_____

_____

5. What will happen if you don't do the task?

_____

_____

_____

6. Are you choosing to do this task or doing it as a hair-trigger reaction to something?

_____

_____

_____

7. If you delay doing the task by 20 minutes, will your choice be different? Why or why not?

_____

_____

_____

8. Does this action feel compulsive or well-thought-out? How so?

_____

_____

_____

9. After answering these questions, do you think this is a true form of self-care? Why or why not?

_____

_____

_____

6

Boundary Setting

Many clients who struggle with alcohol use didn't grow up with parents who modeled healthy boundaries. The adults in their lives may have been unpredictable, dismissive of their opinions, or struggled to uphold healthy boundaries themselves. As a result, some clients grow up to be people-pleasers who are incapable of saying no to others or standing up for themselves. Other clients learn to close themselves off from others to avoid the possibility of rejection. On a basic level, if a client cannot say no when someone offers them a drink, remove themselves from a triggering situation, or keep alcohol out of their home, it is going to be very difficult for them to stay sober. As a result, it is extremely important for clients with disordered drinking to learn how to set healthy boundaries if they are going to recover.

Although boundaries are a popular topic these days, few clients know the exact definition of a boundary or how to apply one to their lives. At its core, a boundary is a guideline or limit that a client creates to signify what they are and are not comfortable with. There are three styles of boundaries that a client can exhibit: rigid, healthy, or porous. These boundaries fall on a spectrum, with rigid boundaries being the firmest and strongest, porous boundaries being the loosest and most open, and healthy boundaries lying somewhere in between.

When clients have rigid boundaries, it's like they are putting up a thick wooden door. Things cannot get in or out, but unlike a wall, clients can choose to open the door and let someone in. In contrast, porous boundaries are the equivalent of a door with large holes in it. Clients with these boundaries often don't have control over how much or how quickly things come in and out. They will often say yes when they want to say no, leading them to feel resentful toward others and causing them to explode later. Finally, healthy boundaries are like a screen door. Clients can filter what comes in and out, while also being flexible (since the screen has some give to it) as needed. Most people have a mix of rigid, porous, and healthy boundaries depending on the person they're interacting with and the situation.

When it comes to understanding your client's alcohol use, it's helpful to examine how these three boundary styles can show up in the same situation. Let's say your client has been sober for a few weeks and is out on the town with a friend who offers them a drink. If they have porous boundaries in this situation, it will likely be hard for them to say no. They may feel guilty about disappointing their friend and think to themselves, *Well, I will just start over again tomorrow. No big deal.* They may also feel tempted to say yes to the drink but then pretend to sip it to avoid asserting their boundaries. On the other hand, if your client has rigid boundaries, they may insult their friend or even cut this person out of their life entirely for not remembering that they were trying to stop drinking. Finally, if your client has healthy boundaries, they might simply tell their friend, "No thank you. I'm actually not drinking right now. I'm not sure when I plan on drinking again, so it would help if you didn't ask me again."

The goal is to help clients identify with whom and in what situations they have different boundaries so they can take action to create as many healthy boundaries as possible. You'll want to help clients firm up porous boundaries and relax more rigid ones. Although clients sometimes worry that they are being selfish by setting healthy boundaries, *boundaries are not selfish*. They give clients a way to show others how they want to be treated and allow them to express their needs, wants, and limitations. Clients cannot expect other people to read their minds. By voicing their wants and needs, they strengthen their relationships and avoid falling into the trap of resentment, gossip, dishonesty, and blame. However, if clients never learned how to set boundaries, they are more likely to drink to avoid the discomfort of having their boundaries crossed or to numb themselves from the pain of not asking for what they need.

Discover Your Boundary Style

Boundaries are limits that you set for yourself and for others. They allow you to be discerning about who can come in and out of your life and what you will (or will not) tolerate in your relationships. There are three general boundary styles: rigid, porous, and healthy. Below are some common signs and symptoms of each. Read through the list and check off any behaviors that you relate to.

Rigid Boundaries	Healthy Boundaries	Porous Boundaries
☐ You become aggressive or give people the silent treatment when frustrated with them.	☐ If someone pushes back when you say no, you understand this doesn't mean that you should have said yes.	☐ You often feel guilty and responsible for how others feel.
☐ You are extremely independent.	☐ You are able to maintain your own sense of self while listening to other people's opinions.	☐ You feel resentful of others, especially when they ask for what they need.
☐ You were raised in a family where keeping things "in the family" was highly important.	☐ You are able to respect others when they say no.	☐ You struggle to voice your opinion.
☐ You avoid close relationships and keep others at a distance.	☐ If someone responds negatively to something you say, you don't automatically assume that you did something wrong.	☐ You feel like other people continuously break their word.
☐ People may describe you as detached, protective, mysterious, or closed off.	☐ When someone shares something with you, you do not automatically reciprocate.	☐ You become overly involved in other people's issues.
☐ You have extremely high expectations of others.	☐ You feel comfortable standing up for yourself when needed.	☐ You feel dependent on other people's approval or acceptance.
☐ You never witnessed your caregivers engage in healthy conflict as a child; everything happened behind closed doors.	☐ You don't put other people's needs above your own well-being.	☐ You tend to overshare.
☐ Your caregivers often told you "because I said so" when they set a boundary with you.	☐ You honestly and clearly communicate your expectations with others.	☐ You feel overwhelmed with all your responsibilities.
☐ You have a history of cutting people off or ghosting them if they do something that upsets you.	☐ You don't compromise your values for others.	☐ You are a people-pleaser and have trouble saying no to requests.
		☐ You often feel like you give people too many chances.
		☐ Your caregivers struggled to say no to you or set limits.

Which boundary style had the most check marks in it? Is this the boundary style that you relate to the most? Why or why not?

_____

_____

_____

_____

Understanding Boundary Styles in Your Life

Now that you have a better understanding of porous, healthy, and rigid boundaries, let's understand how each of these boundary styles shows up in your life. Look through the relationship categories listed here, and circle the most common boundaries you have with the different people in your life. Describe at least one example of how this boundary manifests in each type of relationship.

Friends: Porous   Healthy   Rigid

Provide an example of how this shows up in your life:

_____

_____

_____

Extended family: Porous   Healthy   Rigid

Provide an example of how this shows up in your life:

_____

_____

_____

Immediate family: Porous   Healthy   Rigid

Provide an example of how this shows up in your life:

_____

_____

_____

Significant other: Porous   Healthy   Rigid

Provide an example of how this shows up in your life:

_____

_____

_____

Work colleagues: Porous   Healthy   Rigid

Provide an example of how this shows up in your life:

_____

_____

_____

Your children: Porous   Healthy   Rigid

Provide an example of how this shows up in your life:

_____

_____

_____

With yourself: Porous   Healthy   Rigid

Provide an example of how this shows up in your life:

_____

_____

_____

Types of Boundaries

Now that we have examined different boundary styles, let's take a closer look at the six main types of boundaries: material, physical, temporal, sexual, mental, and emotional. As you discuss these different boundaries with your clients, it is likely that they will have experienced boundary violations in many categories. That's because our society and culture do not prioritize and respect people's boundaries. We live in a world where gaslighting, catcalling, and microaggressions are often the norm. People are conditioned to pretend that everything is okay and turn a blind eye when transgressions occur. It's rare to encounter families, systems, and organizations where meetings start and end on time, consent is explicitly discussed, and people take responsibility for their mistakes and accept feedback. I believe this is especially important to point out because boundary conversations tend to overemphasize the importance of personal responsibility when, in fact, there are also societal factors at play that make it difficult for clients to implement and follow through with setting boundaries.

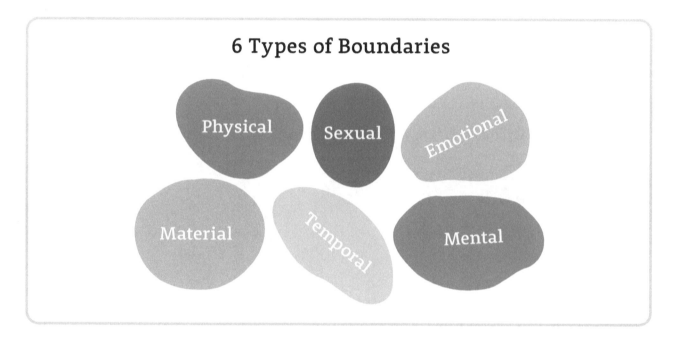

In discussing the six different types of boundaries, clients may also come to realize that they have perpetrated boundary violations themselves. When clients are in a cycle of overdrinking, it's common for them to have difficulty accepting no as an answer, and they may push other people's boundaries without realizing it. This is where it is helpful to remind clients that shame will only make it harder to change. To get sober or change their relationship with alcohol, they must face what they have been avoiding. They can learn from the examples of boundary violations here, take accountability when they violate someone's boundaries, and do better in the future.

Material Boundaries

Material boundaries refer to the limits that clients set when it comes to space and their possessions, such as their money, home, furniture, jewelry, and so on. These boundaries can involve something as small as deciding to share a bottle of water with someone, but it can also involve determining whether to allow certain people into their home. Material boundaries can also refer to the limits that clients have when it comes to what they will (and will not) keep in their home.

Clients who struggle with disordered drinking often need to set material boundaries around alcohol, such as not keeping any form of alcohol in the home. Even if it is not their preferred choice of alcohol, clients can be tempted to drink it if it is in their vicinity, especially if they live alone. Clients will also need to learn to set material boundaries with pushy friends or family members who try to offer them alcohol or engage in other problematic behaviors, such as borrowing money or personal items without their permission.

Clients can experience boundary violations in this area if someone:

- Continues to try to make them drink after the client has said no

- Steals or borrows something from the client without their permission

- Gifts or brings the client a bottle of champagne

- Sends the client a care package with items they know the client cannot have

- Eats food off the client's plate without their permission

- Borrows money from the client and never pays it back

Material Boundaries

Material boundaries refer to limits around your physical possessions, including whom and what you allow in your home, as well as what material items you are willing to share. It is likely that your boundaries will be different with different people. Use this worksheet to identify the material boundaries you already have and which ones you would like to implement to support your recovery.

Below is a list of common material boundaries. Check off any boundaries that you currently set in your life:

☐ Abstaining from alcohol (always, sometimes, or at specific places)

☐ Not lending money to people who don't pay you back

☐ Not accepting physical gifts from people who use them to manipulate you (e.g., a friend who buys you gifts and expects favors in return)

☐ Maintaining an alcohol-free home

☐ Choosing not to share clothing, jewelry, or other belongings with people who damage them or don't return them

☐ Only letting reliable people drive your car

☐ Only letting close friends stay in your home

☐ Only sharing your bed with a committed partner

☐ Not sharing food (always, sometimes, or with specific people)

☐ Not letting your partner go through your phone without your permission

☐ Other: _____

How has your alcohol use affected your material boundaries? Has it affected your ability to set boundaries? Has it contributed to more boundary violations in this area?

_____

_____

_____

_____

What are some material boundaries that would support you in not drinking?

_____

_____

_____

_____

Physical Boundaries

Physical boundaries have to do with a client's comfort level with touch and personal space. It can also involve limits on the people they spend time with and feel safe around, in addition to what places they physically go. It is healthy and normal for clients to have different boundaries with different people in their lives depending on their closeness and comfort. There is nothing right or wrong about how much touch or closeness a client feels comfortable with. They get to choose what works for them based on their experiences and the world around them.

For example, clients with a history of trauma may need more physical space or feel uncomfortable with physical touch, even if the trauma itself didn't involve a boundary violation. Likewise, someone from a marginalized group may not feel comfortable going certain places because they feel like it puts them physically at risk. While no client should have to endure this experience—and our society needs to do more to protect those with the least power—clients have a right to take care of themselves and do what works for them. They are not "overreacting" just because other people, especially those with more privilege, don't understand their physical boundaries.

Many clients may struggle with physical boundaries if they were not taught as children that they have a right to their body and to physical space. They may have been forced to give hugs or physical affection, or had family members constantly entering their room and invading their privacy. In addition, when someone lives in a body that is often ignored, discounted, or violated, they can experience boundary violations either explicitly (through unwanted touch) or implicitly (by not being able to use a bathroom on a plane due to their body size). While being touched by a stranger is a boundary violation for almost any of us, for many clients, this can also reflect a microaggression, such as when a person touches the hair of a Black woman.

Clients can experience violations to their physical boundaries if:

- They are in the presence of someone who is trying to convince them to drink
- They are coerced to go to a bar or another establishment where they are uncomfortable
- They have been physically abused
- They were deprived of physical touch, especially as a child
- They have been hugged by teachers, mentors, therapists, friends, family members, or strangers without their consent
- They continue to be poked, touched, or tickled after telling someone to stop
- They are unable to use a public bathroom, ride an elevator, or find a ramp due to a lack of disability accommodations
- They are unable to sit in a chair in public, eat at a restaurant, sit on a plane, sit on a bus, or get in an MRI machine because their body size is not accommodated

Physical Boundaries

Physical boundaries involve limits around whom you interact with, what kind of physical touch you feel comfortable with, and the places you physically go. It is normal to have different types of physical boundaries with different people in your life based on your level of closeness and comfort. Use this worksheet to identify the physical boundaries you already have and which ones you would like to implement to support your recovery.

Below is a list of common physical boundaries. Check off any boundaries that you currently set in your life:

- ☐ Not shaking hands with strangers
- ☐ Only hugging people in your family (with whom you are comfortable)
- ☐ Not drinking alcohol
- ☐ Needing personal space when sitting on the couch with others
- ☐ Taking a different route home from work so you don't pass your favorite bar
- ☐ Asking people to knock on your door when it's closed
- ☐ Only sharing a bed with your partner
- ☐ Not going to certain restaurants or public places where you are unsure if your body will be treated with respect and dignity
- ☐ Skipping an event because you don't feel safe being around someone there
- ☐ Not sitting close to someone in a public place, if possible, due to the potential of being touched
- ☐ Not going to certain places where you feel uncomfortable, such as a bar or casino
- ☐ Other: _____

How has your alcohol use affected your physical boundaries? Has it affected your ability to set boundaries? Has it contributed to more boundary violations in this area?

_____

_____

_____

What are some physical boundaries that would support you in not drinking?

_____

_____

_____

_____

Temporal Boundaries

Temporal boundaries are the limits that clients place on how much time and energy they spend with others and themselves. It essentially refers to how clients choose to spend their time. When clients have healthy temporal boundaries, they know what drains them and depletes their energy, which allows them to say yes to the things that are important to them and leave out all the rest. Clients who are people-pleasers often struggle with temporal boundaries because they fear that others will become angry, disappointed, or critical if they speak their minds. For example, a client's friend may show up late to a coffee date for the fifth time in a row, but instead of addressing the issue, the client may simply make a passive-aggressive comment and allow their resentment to grow. Another client may always spend late nights at the office because they fear they will be fired if they do not say yes to every extra project their boss asks them to do.

Many clients who are people-pleasers use alcohol to tolerate the discomfort and stress of people breaking their temporal boundaries. They swallow their pride and chase it with alcohol to pretend like they are not bothered by these boundary violations. However, if they want to change their relationship with alcohol, they will need to start protecting their time and energy instead of appeasing others. For example, rather than always accommodating other people's schedules, they will need to designate specific times where they will attend to work, family, and life responsibilities and then carve out protected time for their own pursuits. They will also need to be honest with others by communicating what temporal boundary violations bother them (e.g., running late) instead of expecting others to read their minds.

> **Clients can experience violations to their temporal boundaries if:**
>
> - People insist that they stay longer at a meeting, event, or gathering
>
> - Scheduled events, appointments, or classes do not start or end on time
>
> - The people in their lives are always running late
>
> - People ask the client for support or assistance but do not return the favor
>
> - People do not listen to the client when they say that they don't have the time or energy to do something
>
> - Their job often forces them to stay late or work longer hours than agreed upon without compensation or consent

Temporal Boundaries

Temporal boundaries reflect how a person uses their time. Many individuals do not recognize that temporal boundaries are a very valid and important limit to have in your life, especially if you are trying to heal from an addictive pattern such as drinking. Use this worksheet to identify the temporal boundaries you already have and which ones you would like to implement to support your recovery.

Below is a list of common temporal boundaries. Check off any boundaries that you currently set in your life:

☐ Not staying late after work

☐ Setting limits on the time you spend with people who are chronically late or cancel often

☐ Asking people to call or text before they come over instead of popping in unannounced

☐ Scheduling time to be alone versus always spending time with others

☐ Not overcommitting yourself

☐ Not participating in one-sided relationships

☐ Scheduling time to recover after doing things that are draining

☐ Saying no when you don't have the time or energy to do something

☐ Other: _____

How has your alcohol use affected your temporal boundaries? Has it affected your ability to set boundaries? Has it contributed to more boundary violations in this area?

_____

_____

_____

_____

What are some temporal boundaries that would support you in not drinking?

_____

_____

_____

_____

Sexual Boundaries

Sexual boundaries are the personal limits that clients have around what they will and will not do sexually. This not only includes the types of sexual acts that clients are comfortable with (as well as with whom they are comfortable doing these acts), but also conversations around sexuality, consent, contraception, and sexually transmitted infections (STIs). For clients in committed relationships, sexual boundaries can also reflect how each person in the relationship defines cheating. Many clients who struggle with sexual boundaries may have never had proper sexual education from their caregivers or in school. It can be a powerful exercise to teach them about sexual boundaries, consent, and their rights.

While many people think sexual boundaries and sexual consent are the same thing, there is an important difference. Sexual consent simply reflects a person's agreement to participate in a given sexual activity. Whether or not they give consent is a function of the sexual boundaries that they hold. For example, if a client has sexual boundaries against having intercourse with multiple partners, then they would not consent to engage in a threesome. Consent is also an ongoing process. A client can consent to a certain sexual activity and decide during the course of the activity that they are not comfortable and tell their partner to stop. This does not mean that their boundaries have changed but that consent is an active and continuous process.

For clients who engage in disordered drinking, consent can often become blurry. For example, when a client is under the influence, it can impair their ability to give consent because they are not able to think clearly. They may also allow someone to cross their sexual boundaries, or they may engage in a sexual act that they never would have consented to if they were sober. As you discuss sexual boundaries with your clients, including which ones have been crossed, they may feel shame. It is very common for clients, especially women with alcohol use issues, to beat themselves up for past sexual encounters. They may feel as though they "deserved" what happened to them because they were drunk. It is important to remind them that regardless of how intoxicated they were, this does not give other people a right to violate their sexual boundaries.

Clients can experience violations to their sexual boundaries if:

- They were sexually abused, raped, molested, or harassed

- They were cat-called or told to "smile" by a stranger (especially in the case of a man saying this to a woman)

- Someone made an inappropriate sexual remark to them

- Someone sent the client a naked picture or a sexually explicit image without their consent

- They were pressured, bullied, or cajoled (either explicitly or implicitly) into doing certain sexual acts

- Someone did not ask for the client's consent before engaging in a sexual act with them

- Someone did not use protection when having sex

Sexual Boundaries

Sexual boundaries involve what types of sexual acts, sexual touch, and sexual conversations you are willing engage in. This also includes issues related to consent, contraception, STI protection, definitions of cheating and exclusivity, and so on. Alcohol use often interferes with sexual boundaries and leads people to do things that they are uncomfortable with or later regret. Use this worksheet to identify the sexual boundaries you already have and which ones you would like to implement to support your recovery.

Below is a list of common sexual boundaries. Check off any boundaries that you currently set in your life:

☐ Consenting and asking for consent before beginning sexual activity

☐ Communicating your sexual interests and comfort level with your partner

☐ Asking your partner to use protection

☐ Using contraception

☐ Not feeling comfortable with public displays of affection (PDA)

☐ Not engaging in sexual acts while under the influence of drugs or alcohol

☐ Saying no to sexual acts that make you want to drink or use drugs

☐ Saying no to sexual acts that you are not comfortable with

☐ Not allowing people to call you certain sexual names

☐ Having a safe word

☐ Discussing with your partner what you consider to be cheating

☐ Other: _____

How has your alcohol use affected your sexual boundaries? Has it affected your ability to set boundaries? Has it contributed to more boundary violations in this area?

_____

_____

_____

_____

What are some sexual boundaries that could support you in not drinking?

_____

_____

_____

_____

Mental Boundaries

Mental boundaries refer to the topics of conversation that someone is willing to engage in and with whom. They essentially reflect how willing a person is to share their thoughts, ideas, and opinions with others. When someone has healthy mental boundaries, they can be respectful of other people's opinions without being dismissive or insulting. Clients who are trying to quit drinking will need to set mental boundaries around the topics of alcohol and sobriety. For example, if a friend is always making jokes about blacking out, or a family member is encouraging them to drink despite their desire to stay sober, they will need to a have a frank conversation with the other person. If the individual continues to disrespect the client's boundaries, they may need to limit time spent with them.

Mental boundaries can also extend to content that clients engage with online, including the accounts that they follow on social media. Given the number of accounts that glorify drinking culture, make light of hangovers, and dismiss problematic drinking behaviors, clients who want a healthy relationship with alcohol need to create healthy boundaries by unfollowing these accounts. Alcohol companies also directly market their products through targeted ads on social media, so I recommend having clients go into their settings and directly block ads for alcohol. They may also have friends they follow on these platforms who showcase their unhealthy drinking behavior, in which case the "mute" button can be helpful, which allows clients to still follow these accounts but not have their posts or stories show up in their feed. However, if the other person is solely a drinking buddy, it may be helpful for the client to simply unfriend or unfollow their account.

Mental boundary violations are some of the most common, as they occur when someone disrespects a client's point of view or blatantly gaslights the client in an attempt to make them question their reality. They can also occur in the form of microaggressions, in which clients are subjected to verbal slights surrounding their gender, race, class, ethnicity, socioeconomic status, and more. For example, due to racist stereotypes, it is common for people to assume that any person of color with an addiction is addicted to street drugs instead of alcohol. Clients of color are also more likely to be accused of having legal problems. If you are a white provider, it is incredibly important to take your client's experiences of racism and marginalization seriously. Do not dismiss their concerns or accuse them of being too sensitive. Take anti-racism courses in addition to cultural competence trainings. Do not expect clients of color to educate you. Often, their substance use is a way they cope with the racism and oppression they experience on a daily basis. As a result, make sure they know that they have a right to not engage with certain people who do not respect them or who make them feel "crazy." Until our society improves how we treat people with marginalized identities, boundaries are essential for them.

Clients can experience violations to their mental boundaries if:

- People insist that the client can drink even after they have said they can't or don't

- Other people belittle or put down the client's opinions

- They grew up in a household where adults did not acknowledge any issues that were going on (e.g., a caregiver was often drunk or unavailable, but this was never discussed or acknowledged)

- Someone insults or demeans the client

- They are the victim of racism, homophobia, transphobia, sexism, or xenophobia

- They are frequently subjected to microaggressions or gaslighting tactics

- They grew up in a household where there were strict rules about what they could talk about to people outside the family (e.g., "What happens in the home stays in the home")

- They grew up in a household where multiple perspectives or ideas were not tolerated

- Their experience, opinions, ideas, or thoughts are continuously invalidated, leading them to question themselves

- Someone tells that client that they are "crazy" or says, "You don't know what you're talking about"

- People use God, religion, or spirituality as an excuse to control the client or get them to behave in a certain way

Mental Boundaries

Mental boundaries refer to the conversations, thoughts, and ideas you are willing to entertain and with whom. Setting mental boundaries protects your peace by ensuring you are not subjected to conversations that may be triggering or cause frustration. Mental boundaries are extremely important if you are trying to change your relationship with alcohol because when you are triggered, it puts you at greater risk of drinking. Use this worksheet to identify the mental boundaries you already have and which ones you would like to implement to support your recovery.

Below is a list of common mental boundaries. Check off any boundaries that you currently set in your life:

- ☐ Removing yourself from conversations that have to do with drinking or alcohol
- ☐ Not spending time with individuals who encourage you to drink or think you don't "really" have a problem with alcohol
- ☐ Keeping certain topics off limits (e.g., religion, politics) when interacting with certain people
- ☐ Avoiding any content on television or social media that glorifies drinking
- ☐ Not talking about certain topics at work
- ☐ Not debating strangers or trolls on social media
- ☐ Staying true to your own values and beliefs even when others disagree
- ☐ Distancing yourself from people who gaslight you
- ☐ Other: _____

How has your alcohol use affected your mental boundaries? Has it affected your ability to set boundaries? Has it contributed to more boundary violations in this area?

_____

_____

_____

_____

What are some mental boundaries that could support you in not drinking?

_____

_____

_____

_____

Emotional Boundaries

Emotional boundaries refer to the limits that clients set when it comes to sharing, honoring, and respecting their feelings. At their core, emotional boundaries are intended to protect a client's emotional health. It is important for clients to understand that emotional boundaries do not protect them from feeling their emotions; they simply give them more control over when and where they are willing to process or confront certain emotions. For example, a client may ask to remove themselves from a conversation before it becomes too heated and eventually return to the conversation when both parties have cooled off. Other clients may want to avoid discussing certain topics in public, such as not talking about their recent breakup at the upcoming family gathering.

Emotional boundaries also involve the ability to not take on other people's feelings. This can be difficult for many clients, especially those who grew up in families where there was intense parental conflict, and clients felt responsible for making their parents get along. Clients can also struggle with emotional boundaries if they are not in tune with how they feel. This can occur if clients were raised in a family where emotions were not welcome or their caregivers were not emotionally available. These clients may have learned to suppress their emotions, thus impacting their ability to set emotional boundaries.

If someone is in a marginalized group, emotional boundaries can unfortunately look like choosing to not go to certain places to ensure they won't be bullied, harassed, or teased. For example, clients of color may not feel safe going to certain neighborhoods or traveling to areas that are predominantly white. Trans and gender-expansive individuals may not want to risk going to certain venues where they will have to use a public restroom and be at risk for being publicly harassed. Clients in large bodies may not want to go to the gym out of fear of ridicule. As a clinician, it is important to validate the injustice of these experiences and be a support system for your client. The reality is that our systems need to change so the burden of protecting oneself does not always fall on those with the least power. However, until this happens, clients have a right to advocate for themselves and set strong boundaries in order to protect their peace and take care of their emotional well-being.

Clients can experience emotional boundary violations if:

- Their caregivers treated them like a therapist or friend while growing up

- Their caregivers triangulated them and put them in the middle of their relationship

- People unload their struggles onto the client without asking if they have the capacity to listen and be present

- People gossip to the client about their close friends, putting them in the middle

- Someone is not emotionally present or validating when the client shares something deeply emotional or sensitive

- They were emotionally neglected by their family or told not to talk about their feelings

- They were shamed or bullied for any reason, especially for their weight, gender, sexual orientation, race, ability, appearance, or religion

Emotional Boundaries

Emotional boundaries involve the limits that you set when it comes to sharing certain personal information, including how quickly you share that information and under what circumstances. When you have healthy emotional boundaries, you are mindful of your emotions, you ask for what you need, and you don't take on other people's emotions as your own. If you drink in response to uncomfortable or painful emotions, emotional boundaries are going be very important in your recovery. Use this worksheet to identify the emotional boundaries you already have and which ones you would like to implement to support your recovery.

Below is a list of common emotional boundaries. Check off any boundaries that you currently set in your life:

☐ Taking time to cool off after an argument

☐ Asking to revisit a difficult conversation when you are in a better mood

☐ Only sharing your feelings with people who respect you

☐ Standing up for yourself and not allowing people to shame or belittle you

☐ Not talking about topics that will upset you and trigger you to drink

☐ Letting people know when you're not in a place to listen to them

☐ Choosing not to answer personal questions when you don't know someone very well

☐ Understanding that other people's emotions are not your responsibility

☐ Avoiding places where you are unsure if you will be bullied or harassed due to your race, gender, sexual orientation, class, religion, ability, weight, etc.

☐ Other: _____

How has your alcohol use affected your emotional boundaries? Has it affected your ability to set boundaries? Has it contributed to more boundary violations in this area?

_____

_____

_____

_____

What are some emotional boundaries that could support you in not drinking?

_____

_____

_____

_____

How to Communicate Boundaries

Once you've explained the concept of boundaries to a client, it's time to help them communicate these boundaries to others. You can do so by teaching them the following two-prong approach: (1) Clearly set the limit, and (2) State the consequence that will occur if this limit is violated. However, if this is a client's first time setting a boundary regarding a particular issue, they may want to refrain from immediately imposing a consequence and instead see if the other person respects their boundary first. If the situation keeps arising, then the client can state the consequence so the person can make an informed choice about how to proceed. Here are some examples:

- **Material:** "Please do not take my pen without asking. If you do this again, I am not going to be able to study with you."

- **Physical:** "I am not comfortable with you touching my hair. I am not going to be able to spend time with you if you cannot respect this boundary."

- **Temporal:** "I only have 20 minutes to talk on the phone. After that, I need to go spend time with my family."

- **Sexual:** "I do not have sex without using protection. If you continue to ask me to do this, we are not going to be able to spend time together anymore."

- **Mental:** "Please do not talk about my weight. If you continue to make comments like this, I will not be able to spend time with you."

- **Emotional:** "I do not feel comfortable answering that question. Please do not ask me again. If you continue to ask me this, I won't be able to share intimate details of my life with you."

Although this two-prong approach can be effective on its own—especially when clients want to set a strict boundary with someone they don't know very well—clients can sometimes get pushback if they set a boundary for the first time without giving any context. In these cases, the other person may want to defend themselves and share how their intentions were good. They may be offended or not understand where this boundary came from. They may accuse the client of being mean. When this happens, clients can make the other person more receptive by changing some phrasing and describing their reasons for setting the boundary. In particular, clients can (1) Acknowledge that the boundary represents a change from the status quo; and/or (2) Relay their understanding that the other person has good intentions. They can also offer an alternative instead of a consequence, though this will depend on how important the boundary is to the client.

- **Acknowledge:** "I know in the past I have not said anything about _____. However, I am realizing that I am actually uncomfortable with it."

- **Understand:** "I know you love me/care about me/have good intentions when you say or do _____. At the same time, it does not work for me when you say or do _____."

- **Set the limit:** "Please do not do or say _____."
- **State the consequence or offer an alternative:** "If you do _____ again, I will do _____." or "Could we do _____ instead?"

Here are some examples of how these boundaries can look in practice:

- **Material:** "I know in the past I have been fine with sharing clothes. However, I'm realizing that I am actually uncomfortable with it. Please do not ask if you can borrow my clothes in the future."

- **Physical:** "I know you love me and care about me, which is why you want to be close to me. However, I need some physical space right now instead of sitting so close to you on the couch. Can we please sit a little farther apart or cuddle later?"

- **Temporal:** "I love how close we are. At the same time, I get overwhelmed when you call me a few times in a row. Unfortunately, I do not have time to talk on the phone every day. How about we set up a recurring time to chat once a week?"

- **Sexual:** "I know you want to hold my hand in public because you care about me and are proud to be with me. At the same time, I am really uncomfortable with PDA. I am happy to hold your hand at home or in private."

- **Mental:** "I know you love me, but at the same time, I have different political beliefs than you. I am not comfortable talking about politics and will need to limit the time I spend with you if you continue to talk about them."

- **Emotional:** "Mom and Dad, I know I haven't spoken up in the past, but the truth is I am realizing it is very uncomfortable for me to hear you vent about each other. Please seek outside support. I am happy to talk to you guys about anything else, but I can no longer be in the middle."

As you work together to help clients communicate boundaries with others, make sure they aren't putting pressure on themselves to create the "perfect boundary"—because perfect boundaries do not exist. If this is their first time setting boundaries with someone, they may not be able to fully communicate their desired boundary in one conversation. Sometimes it takes a few conversations to get their point across. In addition, boundaries need to be maintained over time. Just like clients may need to clean or repaint a door, they will need to put work in to make sure their boundaries stay healthy and true to what they need depending on what is going on in their lives.

> **Quick Tip:** Guilt is the most common reason people avoid setting a boundary. They fear that the other person will feel bad or be upset. They think that they are rude or unsympathetic if they are honest. However, the truth is other people's feelings are not the client's responsibility. The client is simply responsible for setting the boundary, but they are not responsible for how the other person feels. Their goal is to protect their own peace.

Setting a Boundary

Setting a boundary can feel scary and overwhelming at first. Sometimes you might feel at a loss for words and forget what you are trying to say. However, it gets easier with practice. Use this worksheet to identify a boundary you'd like to implement, and write out exactly what you would like to say to the other person. Then examine the costs and payoffs of not setting this boundary. This will help you build motivation to set this boundary sooner rather than later.

Think of a boundary that you would like to set with someone in your life. Use the following framework to communicate your boundary to this person.

1. Acknowledge that the boundary represents a change in the relationship: _____

_____

2. Tell the other person that you understand their intentions: _____

_____

3. Set the limit: _____

_____

4. State the consequence or offer an alternative: _____

_____

After writing out how you would like to set your boundary, practice stating it out loud. Bonus points for practicing in the mirror. Sometimes we write differently than we speak, and if you say the words out loud, it will feel less awkward when you set the boundary in real life. When you're done, write down any thoughts, feelings, or fears that come up when you think about setting this boundary.

_____

_____

_____

What is it costing you to not set this boundary? For example, it is eating away at your time, energy, peace of mind, or connection to this person?

_____

_____

_____

_____

What is the payoff of not setting this boundary? For example, is it allowing you to avoid vulnerability, to sidestep potential conflict, or to avoid taking responsibility?

_____

_____

_____

_____

Now practice setting this boundary sometime this week. Describe how it went, including how you feel before, during, and after setting the boundary. Was the other person receptive? What was the outcome?

_____

_____

_____

_____

If your interaction didn't go as well as you'd hoped, remember that just because someone pushes back on your boundary doesn't mean you should not have set it. The boundary is there to protect *you*, not the other person. In addition, know that boundaries get easier with practice. You will have many more opportunities to practice setting limits so you can get your needs met.

Boundaries at Family Events

The longer your client has been in a relationship with someone, the more difficult it is to change the dynamic or the status quo, which is why family dynamics are often some of the most difficult ones to change. After all, clients have known many of these people since birth! Therefore, your client should expect pushback whenever they challenge the family culture—for example, by deciding not to participate in holiday drinking games. This pushback isn't necessarily a reflection of the fact that the family doesn't care about the client; rather, they are used to them doing things a certain way and don't want them to change. Even in the face of this resistance, clients should not give up. If they avoid setting boundaries, they will only cause themselves a greater headache down the road because they are not actually facing the problem head-on.

It's important to remind clients that when they set boundaries, they are taking care of their future selves. It may be more work upfront, but eventually people are more likely to respect their boundary (and may even start to support them by serving seltzer at the family BBQ), which will never happen if clients only cope with their family by avoiding them. Clients don't need to attend every family gathering or even stay the whole time—especially if they are new on this journey or very easily triggered—but if they want to live a life that they don't have to escape from, they will need to have these tough conversations and decide how to handle family events.

Coping with Family Gatherings and Events

One of the most common issues that prevents people from questioning their relationship with alcohol is the fear of how they will handle family gatherings and events. Family members can be some of the most difficult people to set boundaries with because you may feel embarrassed to discuss your reasons for getting sober, or there may already be an established culture of drinking in the family. This worksheet will help you identify how you can make family gatherings more comfortable and help you develop a plan to use if you need to remove yourself from the situation.

1. **Suggest an alternative.** This may not always be possible, but if you are included in the planning process, suggest something that is not completely alcohol focused. Often, people get stuck in doing the same few things. Maybe they haven't thought about taking a cooking class or going on a hike. Even if you can't influence the plans, see if there is an activity you can bring. Does your family always do the same thing for holidays? Bring a board game or a craft so you will have something to do beyond drinking.

   What are some alternatives you can try? List out common family activities and a possible alternative for each.

Family Activity	Alternative
_____	_____
_____	_____
_____	_____
_____	_____

2. **Make a plan.** Decide beforehand whether you will be drinking at the gathering. If you are not, I recommend making sure at least one person knows so they can support you. Tell them before you go, if possible, so you get the difficult conversation over with beforehand. The event may be difficult enough for you as it is without having to explain to other people that you are questioning your relationship with alcohol. At the same time, be prepared for people to ask why you aren't drinking. Think through different scenarios and practice exactly how you will respond so you feel more comfortable.

3. **Think about your beverages.** Can you bring your own soda in case they don't have anything you like? If you are going to a wedding, how are you going to handle the toast? Bartenders are often happy to make you a mocktail based on the signature drink (whether this is a wedding or at a bar). If you like mocktails, going to a bar that has a good cocktail menu is often a good sign that they can make you a decent mocktail, especially compared to a dive bar.

What nonalcoholic beverage could you bring to the next family party?

_____

_____

_____

4. **Find a job.** Sometimes if you feel awkward at a gathering, the best thing you can do is keep busy! Offer to help with cooking, cleaning, organizing, or even watching the kids.

What is a job you could do at the next family gathering?

_____

_____

_____

5. **Take breaks.** Sometimes you don't need to leave the gathering; you just need a break. If your mom says something that frustrates you or people start taking shots in the kitchen, change your environment. Walk into another room. Take a few minutes in the bathroom and splash cold water on your face. Head outside for some fresh air. It's unlikely people will even notice you are gone. Give yourself some time to ground yourself and come back when you feel more centered.

How can you take a break during a gathering or event?

_____

_____

_____

6. **Think of your escape route.** Sometimes things go sour, and you need a plan to leave. Can you leave right after dinner if things start getting too rowdy? Can you drive yourself so you aren't dependent on someone else for a ride? People may not understand or like it, but it is better to take care of yourself now and work through their frustration than do something you regret.

What can you do if you need to leave early? How can you take care of yourself?

_____

_____

_____

7

Sober Socializing

The fear of socializing without alcohol is one of the most common reasons that people won't take a break from drinking or quit altogether. Most people cannot imagine having a fulfilling social life without alcohol because they have very few role models in this area. Our society touts alcohol as the preferred way to have fun and bond with others. It's the glue that holds everybody's social lives together: It gives people something to talk about, makes them relatable, and signals to other people that they're cool and don't take themselves too seriously. It's no wonder that so many clients are afraid of being judged if they consider not drinking. They worry that they will feel different from others, especially if they have a tendency toward social anxiety and get easily overwhelmed in interpersonal situations. Many people start drinking in high school, before their brain is fully developed, so they never learn how to meet new people, make friends, network, date, or socialize as an adult without a drink in their hand.

Sober Socializing Inventory

In order to change your relationship with alcohol, it is important to understand how drinking is intertwined with your social life, including your friendships, your family, and even your job. It is also important to break down what fears you have about socializing without alcohol. Fill out the questions below to explore your social relationship with alcohol.

1. How interconnected is drinking with your social life? What role does it play in your friendships? Do you only hang out with your friends at bars or other venues that serve alcohol? When you interact with your friends, is drinking always involved?

_____

_____

_____

2. How interconnected is drinking with family life? What role does it play in your immediate and extended family? Did you grow up with parents who drank every night? Has alcohol use ever driven a wedge between family members?

_____

_____

_____

3. How interconnected is drinking with your work life? Is drinking encouraged at your job (or at work parties or networking events)? Does it play a role in your relationship with your coworkers?

_____

_____

_____

_____

4. Are there certain situations—for example, weddings, holidays, parties—in which you cannot imagine yourself not drinking? Why?

_____

_____

_____

_____

5. What are your fears about quitting drinking? What are you afraid people will think or say to you? Who are you most worried will think or say these things?

_____

_____

_____

_____

6. After reading over the answers to your last two questions, flip back to the "Alcohol History Inventory" from chapter 1, and re-read the words that came up for you when I asked you to think of the word *alcohol* and the word *sober* (or someone who doesn't drink). Is there any overlap between your fears of quitting drinking and your answers on the inventory?

_____

_____

_____

_____

How Clients Can Tell People They Aren't Drinking

When clients are in a social setting where they turn down a drink, the most common response they hear is a resounding "Why?!" People around them may wonder, *Surely this person must have a good reason. Otherwise, they would be drinking!* The dreaded "why" question is difficult for clients to answer because they feel pressured to come up with a good enough excuse that people will accept. Unfortunately, this usually backfires. Let me explain.

While it may be tempting for clients to blame their choice to stay sober on some external factor—such as "I am the designated driver tonight" or "I have to get up early tomorrow because I'm moving"—this is problematic for a few reasons. First, if the client is coming up with a fake excuse, it can feel uncomfortable and bring up shame, especially if they have a history of lying in their addiction. Second, dishonesty may go against their values, which can negatively impact their self-worth. Finally, these excuses only provide the client with a short-term solution to why they aren't drinking *tonight.* They do not solve the larger issue of how the client will continue to say no to a drink in the future. They are simply putting off this conversation, which will only get more awkward as they run out of excuses, making them more likely to drink again in the future.

Instead, it is important that clients try not to blame their lack of drinking on something external. Because in my personal and professional experience, people will go to amazing lengths to solve clients' problem of "not drinking tonight." For example, the most selfish people will suddenly insist on paying for the client's ride home or offer to help them move in the morning. And once they do that, it becomes an awkward situation. Instead, encourage clients to keep it simple and straightforward by using a short phrase that makes not drinking about *them* (e.g., "I choose not to," "I hate hangovers," "I feel better when I don't"), as opposed to something external (e.g., needing to move in the morning or being the designated driver). Encourage them to share something that is vague enough to not invite further questions. And if the other person follows up with the dreaded "why" question again, clients can simply repeat the same phrase again and then change the subject.

At a certain point, though, if clients come to the realization that they want to quit drinking completely, it is helpful for them to tell a few close people. Hiding something can lead to shame. In addition, if clients are always socializing with the same people, such as colleagues at work, it may be helpful for them to share about their sobriety so they don't have to rehash the same conversation every time. This is a boundary that may take more work up front, but clients don't need to refer to themselves as alcoholics in order to stop drinking. Clients don't need to label themselves in any way unless it's helpful. Instead, here are some alternative words they can consider. Discuss with your client what words might feel right for them:

- Sober
- Sober curious
- Nondrinker
- In recovery
- Teetotaler

- Retired drinker
- Retired partier
- On a sober streak
- Alcohol free

Answering the "Why" Question

One of the most common things that prevents people from cutting back on their alcohol use is answering the dreaded "why" question when declining a drink. As a result, it's important to practice how you'll respond to this question—because you will inevitably be asked. Put a check mark by any of the following prompts that you think you could give a try.

- ☐ "I've drank enough for a lifetime."
- ☐ "I choose not to."
- ☐ "I assure you, I have a very good reason [*wink*]."
- ☐ "I feel better when I don't."
- ☐ "I'm in recovery/sober/an alcoholic [or whatever word you like]."
- ☐ "I don't like the person I am when I drink."
- ☐ "Drinking was preventing me from accomplishing my goals."
- ☐ "I hate having hangovers."
- ☐ "It doesn't mix well with my life."
- ☐ "I'm on medication." (I am not the biggest fan of this one because people may ask you what medication and offer you an alternative medication that will let you drink!)
- ☐ "Because when I drink even a small amount, I feel terrible."
- ☐ "I'm focusing on my health right now."
- ☐ "I just don't like it."
- ☐ Share some of your own personal reasons: _____

_____

Out of all of these, pick one or two that resonate with you the most. Write them here.

_____

_____

_____

_____

After writing them down, practice saying these words out loud a few times. I know this may feel corny, but the truth is, the more comfortable you get with your answer, the less awkward you will feel and the less tempted you will be to say yes to a drink when you want to say no. How did it feel to say it aloud or in the mirror?

_____

_____

_____

_____

Helping Clients Reconnect with Themselves

After getting sober, clients are often surprised to learn that what they used to enjoy doing isn't fun anymore without the addition of alcohol to smooth everything over. That's because getting sober is like getting glasses for the first time. People suddenly realize how blurry their vision was. There is a big, vibrant, and colorful world out there—and they weren't seeing it clearly! While this can be exciting because it allows people to start finding joy in the simple things, it can also be a rude awakening as clients realize that their friendships, relationships, job, or hobbies may not be very fulfilling. They may realize that they have social anxiety and have been using alcohol as a crutch. They may realize that a friendship is lackluster and they have been using alcohol as an excuse to connect. These realizations can bring on scary feelings that can unfortunately lead clients right back to drinking. However, it's important for clients to remember that if they continue to drink in an effort to avoid facing themselves, they will not have a meaningful and fulfilling life. Instead, they will continue drinking as a way to have fun or to cope with anxiety, fear, or awkwardness.

Therefore, it's important that clients take the time to get to know themselves again in their sobriety. In considering what they truly enjoy doing, they need to ask themselves, *Do I really like going to a super crowded bar that reeks of beer while people talk over each other? Do I like going to sporting events and hanging out in a parking lot for a few hours before? Do I enjoy spending time with this friend when we don't have drunken nights or interesting cocktails to bond over?* None of these questions have right or wrong answers, but they are important questions for clients to unpack. Maybe it *is* fun to go to a crowded bar—and having a beer is just the cherry on top of an already enjoyable experience. If that's true, it may be helpful to have clients try it sober to make sure it's an enjoyable experience without the booze. However, it is important that clients are ready for this potentially triggering experience. Clients should only consider going to a bar if they are at least six months sober and have not experienced any active cravings for at least 30 days.

Some clients may struggle to identify whether certain activities are enjoyable when alcohol is removed from the scenario. There is some nuance to this, and it may be helpful for them to consider other factors about the social experience that they hadn't thought about before. For example, I still enjoy going to bars if they are not too crowded, and if they have great ambiance and design. However, going to a dive bar isn't worth it or fun for me. I also have a higher tolerance for going to bars where they offer mocktails or kombucha, or if there is an activity to do such as pool or Skee-Ball. Some things though, like wine tasting, are never worth it for me. No matter how beautiful the scenery and ambiance are, I feel way too uncomfortable when I go. I will also never go to a sports game because I truly have zero interest. I avoid networking events at all costs but do enjoy going to classes or events where there is something to do and socializing and drinking are not the only focus.

Help your clients get curious. Their tolerance for events and activities may change over time and depend on who they are with. In addition, the more they practice doing things without alcohol, the more their self-esteem grows as they gain confidence that they don't need alcohol to have fun or be social.

Discover Your Interests

For many adults, drinking alcohol is one of their main hobbies. Whether it's bar hopping, wine tasting, pub crawling, or playing drinking games, there are endless ways to spend time drinking alone or with a group. Fear of boredom is a huge barrier that prevents many people from questioning their relationship with alcohol, so if you want to cut back on drinking or quit altogether, it is important to discover your interests beyond alcohol. Fill out the questions below to start thinking about new hobbies that do not involve drinking.

1. What did you love to do as a child? Did you gravitate toward art, reading, sports, or music? What about cooking, photography, singing, or dancing?

_____

_____

_____

_____

2. What do you currently like to do that doesn't involve alcohol?

_____

_____

_____

_____

3. Have you ever had moments of being so immersed in something that you lost sense of time? If so, what types of activities were you doing when this occurred?

_____

_____

_____

_____

4. What are some things you've done while drinking that you probably would not want to do sober (e.g., staying late in a crowded bar)?

_____

_____

_____

_____

5. What are some activities that you've enjoyed doing that will probably still be fun without alcohol?

_____

_____

_____

_____

Types of Friendships

As clients examine their relationship with alcohol, they may come to the painful realization that some friends are no longer pleasurable to spend time around when alcohol is removed from the equation. They may also realize that they have much more in common with certain people who are eager to do activities with them that extend beyond drinking. Or they may recognize that they need a larger community of sober friends or people who really "get it." Regardless of where your client falls on this spectrum, know that this is a normal process for clients to go through as they navigate sobriety.

In helping clients evaluate what they want out of their relationships, it can be helpful to examine the extent to which the following types of friendships are present in their lives: utility friendships, pleasure friendships, and close friendships. *Utility friendships* are those that are convenient for clients or based on some sort of mutual benefit. This can include study buddies, neighbors, coworkers, and so on. *Pleasure friendships* include the people that clients genuinely enjoy spending time with. While clients may not be particularly close to these individuals, they nonetheless share common hobbies or interests, and they appreciate being in their company. Finally, *close friendships* include the people with whom clients have the deepest bond. These are the closest confidants to whom clients can turn for support and talk to about anything.

Although clients can get caught in the trap of not wanting any utility or pleasure friendships—and just wanting close friendships—having a healthy mix of each type of friendship is ideal. We are all multifaceted human beings who can benefit from a variety of people who can support our different preferences, interests, hobbies, and environment. A helpful rule of thumb is for clients to find at least one close confidant who also understands their journey. Accountability can be an important thing when people are cutting back on drinking, and it is important for clients to have someone they can text if they are triggered or simply need a listening ear.

Apart from that, encourage clients to cultivate more utility and pleasure friendships in their lives. While this may seem counterintuitive since pleasure and utility friendships are more transient, they are also much easier and quicker to make. It takes about 200 hours before we become close friends with someone,[34] which could take years considering that most Americans only spend about 41 minutes each day socializing.[35] Therefore, spending time with acquaintances can help clients achieve a sense of community on a day-to-day basis, especially if they do not live near many close friends. In fact, having numerous acquaintances reduces feelings of loneliness and promotes a sense of happiness and belonging.[36] Therefore, encourage clients to consider how they can cultivate each type of friendship in their lives.

Types of Friendships

Community is critical in recovery. It helps you combat shame, loneliness, and isolation—all of which are important in healing and changing your relationship with alcohol. While many people long for close and deep relationships—and those are certainly important—research shows that acquaintances can also have a big impact in decreasing loneliness. The following worksheet will break down the three types of friendships so you can identify the friends you have in your support system.

Utility friendships: These are the types of friendships where your connection is based on your usefulness to each other. This can include your work friends, business partners, classmates, neighbors, or someone in your field with whom you swap advice. It can also include someone who is close to your best friend, so you are friends with this person simply because you see them often. Maybe this person is sober too. Utility friendships typically do not include people you would necessarily choose to be friends with, but the friendship is mutually beneficial for both parties. Since these friendships are not based on companionship, they tend to be short-lived, and these friendships do not endure if you no longer work together or see each other.

Make a list of the utility friendships that you value:

_____

_____

_____

_____

Pleasure friendships: These are the types of friendships where your connection is based on the enjoyment you derive from each other. These are friends with whom you share the same sense of humor, enjoy the same interests, and have fun engaging in similar hobbies. These may be people you don't see often but to whom you can reach out when you want to grab a coffee or try out a new fitness class. You may not call these friends in an emergency, but you'd still invite them to your birthday party because you genuinely enjoy their company. While these friendships are typically deeper than utility friendships because of the mutual interest and pleasure involved, they can change across time as your idea of fun and pleasure change.

Make a list of the pleasure friendships that you value:

_____

_____

_____

_____

Close friendships: Close friendships are based on mutual love, honesty, admiration, and reciprocity. These are the types of friendships most of us crave. While your close friends may have started as friendships of utility or pleasure, they are now people with whom you have developed a deep connection. This can include a best friend you're in regular contact with, or it can also be the type of person that you don't get a chance to see or talk to often, but when you do, it is as if no time has passed.

Make a list of the close friendships that you value:

_____

_____

_____

_____

Of the utility, pleasure, and close friends that you listed, to whom can you reach out if you need support with your sobriety goals? Are any of the people you listed supportive of your recovery? Are any of them sober (or do some of them not drink much)?

_____

_____

_____

_____

Qualities of Healthy Friendships

Like all things in sobriety, socializing and making friends is going to take more work and effort without alcohol to smooth the awkwardness or anxiety. However, if clients stick with it, the result will be more authentic and deeper connections. That's because without the haze of alcohol, they know themselves better and can recognize what they want and need in a friend. They are also better at seeing people for who they are.

If clients are looking to create deeper connections, encourage them to look for the eight qualities of healthy friendships: honesty, trust, respect, equality, support, autonomy, self-expression, and communication. The backbone of any healthy relationship is *honesty* and *trust*. Honesty does not mean that clients must tell their friends every explicit detail of what they are thinking. Instead, it means that they can be vulnerable and share their perspective with the other person, especially when they have a concern or disagreement. However, vulnerability requires trust. Clients must feel secure enough in the relationship to know that the other person will not share with others what was revealed in confidence.

No healthy relationship is possible without *respect*. People don't have to agree with everything another person says in order to show respect. They simply have to value each other's opinions and appreciate the unique qualities that make them who they are. Sometimes, throughout the recovery process, clients come to the realization that certain friendships are not built on the pillar of mutual respect. For example, a client who cuts back on drinking may have a close friend who continues to party and black out in their presence, suggesting that perhaps this person isn't a friend after all. This is likely to change the nature of the friendship, potentially reducing it to a utility or pleasure friendship, or it may cause the dissolution of the friendship altogether.

Equality is another important characteristic of a close friendship. If one individual values the friendship more than the other, it is going to be difficult to maintain a connection. Having equality in relationships doesn't mean that clients need to rank their friends by order of preference but that each party needs to put forth equal effort to maintain the friendship. However, I commonly find that clients get fixated on making sure the effort in the relationship is split at an even 50/50, whether it comes to texting, socializing, or making plans. The truth is that some individuals are not big on texting, while some love to text. Some individuals are more extraverted, while others are not up for attending big parties. But this does not necessarily mean that the friendship is unequal. It just means that clients need to be honest about their expectations and accept each other's differences. They may find that some friendships are likely worth keeping, even if they don't get to see a particular friend as much as they would like.

In addition to equality, healthy friendships involve mutual *support*, meaning that each person in the relationship is a source of encouragement and assistance for the other person. This can involve providing a listening ear in times of difficulty or doing a favor for the other person as a way to show kindness. Healthy friendships should have a mix of support and *autonomy*, meaning that clients can reach out to a friend when they need someone, but they are also able to have their own life, make their own decisions, and do things on their own. Friendships can become unhealthy if one party becomes possessive of the other or does not allow for individuality. This is why *self-expression* is also an important part of solid friendships. Clients must feel comfortable being themselves around their friends and not fear being judged or mocked for their choices. If a client's friend does not support their sobriety or judges their choices, it is unlikely the two can remain close friends.

Finally, *communication* is what keeps a close friendship alive during the twists and turns of life. Many clients who struggle with alcohol use have poor communication skills, and when conflict arises, they sweep everything under the rug. Others resort to people-pleasing behavior in an attempt to sidestep disagreements. However, in a long-term friendship, conflict is inevitable. It is important to remind clients that they cannot prevent disagreements from happening and that if they spend enough time with someone, they will not see eye-to-eye on everything. In addition, individuals in recovery have likely caused harm in their relationships, so if they want to rekindle these relationships, they will need to apologize and repair any ruptures.

Friendship Questionnaire

As you evaluate the different relationships that you have in your life, the following questions can help you discern whether a particular relationship qualifies as healthy. Keep in mind that you do not need to answer yes to all these questions for the friendship to be healthy, but this exercise will help you discover if it is a relationship worth keeping. You can also grab a notebook and repeat this exercise with as many friends as you need.

Friend: _____

1. Do you look forward to being around this person? How do you feel before, during, and after spending time with them?

   Before: _____

   During: _____

   After: _____

2. Are you able to set boundaries with them? Do they respect your boundaries?

   _____

   _____

   _____

   _____

3. Are you able to disagree and still respect each other? Do you feel like you can be honest with them?

   _____

   _____

   _____

   _____

4. Do you feel like the friendship is reciprocal? (Note: It's possible that not every aspect of the relationship will be equally reciprocal. For example, you may be more of the planner in the relationship and take the reins on organizing get-togethers. However, the other person may be better at remembering your birthday and other important events in your life.)

_____

_____

_____

_____

5. Do you trust them? Do they keep their word?

_____

_____

_____

_____

6. Do you have similar interests or hobbies? Or is there a special bond that makes the relationship important to you? For example, perhaps you have known each other since you were young kids.

_____

_____

_____

_____

7. Do you feel like you can be yourself around this person? Or do you feel pressured to look or act a certain way?

_____

_____

_____

_____

8. If you stop drinking, will this person be supportive of your recovery? Have you spent time with them sober? What is their relationship with alcohol like?

_____

_____

_____

_____

9. After evaluating this, do you think your friendship is healthy? Do you want to continue this relationship?

_____

_____

_____

_____

Making Friends as an Adult

At this point, your client may be wondering, *This is great info, but how do I actually* make *friends as an adult?* Great question. One of the best ways for a client to start making new friends is to tap into people they already know. These can include individuals who frequent the same coffee shop as them, friends of friends, neighbors, or the friendly looking dog-walker they always see at the dog park. Clients may be surprised by the number of people they're familiar with but have yet to talk to.

There may also be people in the client's life with whom they've lost touch and would like to reconnect. Long-lost friends are often a good place to start because the client already has a tie to these individuals, and they don't have to start from scratch. Mutual friends are another untapped resource since clients have the benefit of being introduced to someone that another friend already knows well. Encourage clients to make a list of all the adjacent people they know with whom they would like to be better friends. It can be helpful for them to start with a larger list because some people on that list may not be looking for new friends, while others the client may not connect with.

Clients can also make friends by engaging in their own passions and interests. If they are interested in sports, encourage them to join an intramural league. If they love to work out, have them join a gym or frequent some yoga or exercise studios. If they love the arts, see if there's an art, dance, or improv class they can take. If they love psychology or personal development, help them find a relevant workshop or university class they can sit in on. Do they care about local politics or have an organization they are passionate about supporting? They can go to a rally, attend a meeting, or volunteer their time. You can also encourage clients to ask themselves, *Where would a potential friend be hanging out on a Friday night? What would they be doing on a Saturday afternoon?*—and encourage them to go to that very place or do that very thing.

Once clients begin venturing out and trying new hobbies to meet friends, they can fall into the common trap of giving up if they do not make a connection right away. Consistency is key in trying to make new connections. It often takes going back to the same dog park, yoga class, or coffee shop week after week before a client sees someone they want to spend time with (and before they even feel comfortable enough asking the other person to grab coffee). A helpful rule of thumb is to suggest that your client go somewhere at least three times before they give up on the idea of making friends there. Many clients are also very unskilled and nervous when it comes to making small talk, so it can be helpful to role-play how to do so in session. You can then encourage clients to stay off their phone when they are waiting in line at a coffee shop or grocery store so they can get better at chatting with people they do not know.

Finally, clients can meet friends online. Dating apps are not just for romantic connections anymore. There are dozens of apps that can support clients in making new friends, such as Bumble BFF, Cliq, and Yubo. Many of these apps also match people up with their interests. For example, there are friend apps for new moms, dog owners, and exercise lovers. Clients can also connect with people through social media, which can help them find clubs, meetups, or other in-person events, as well as connect with specific people. However, just like online dating, clients can fall into the trap of only connecting with someone online and never meeting up in person, which prevents the friendship from truly getting off the ground. It is extremely common these days to follow people on social media and keep in casual contact with them but never meet up. Encourage clients to get off the app and meet people in real life.

Making Friends

Making friends as an adult is challenging. However, it is possible. One of the easiest ways to meet friends is to get involved with an activity or group where you can meet a lot of people at once who have similar interests to you. Ask yourself, *Where would my ideal friend be spending time on a Friday night or Saturday afternoon?* Go there. The following checklist gives you some ideas for meeting friends in person and online. Put a check mark by any ideas you might want to try.

Meeting Friends in Person

☐ **Yoga, dance, or exercise studios:** Group fitness classes can be a wonderful place to meet new friends. They encourage community and offer additional workshops or trainings that you can attend and get to know people better. They may also organize gatherings before or after class.

☐ **Personal development workshops:** Are you into tarot? Spirituality? Want to learn better communication skills? There are a wide range of workshops for personal development where you can learn skills and meet people who have similar goals as you. It is admittedly easier to make friends in person, but some virtual workshops may be a way to meet others as well, especially if it is a multi-day workshop.

☐ **Art classes:** Local art studios are a fun way to learn a new craft and meet people with similar interests. You can take a painting or pottery class, or even check out local universities in the area to see if they offer summer art classes.

☐ **Hiking or running clubs:** Many retail stores that sell running shoes or athletic wear offer free community classes or running clubs (e.g., Athleta and Lululemon). These can be a great way to meet people who have similar interests to you.

☐ **Sports or intramural groups:** Did you play a sport in high school or college and now miss it? Many cities have local intramural sports clubs that you can find in your area. These are a great way to get to know people over time (since you will be on a team with them) and connect over a shared interest.

☐ **Networking events:** If you enjoy being around and meeting different types of people, networking events can be a great way to meet friends and build your career. Maybe your high school, college, or fraternity or sorority has reunions. Check out your area to see what types of networking events are going on that you might be interested in attending.

☐ **Book clubs:** Whether they are in person or online, book clubs can be a great way to meet new people. These clubs often meet several times a year, so you can slowly get to know someone before asking them to meet up outside of the scheduled meetings.

☐ **Sober bars:** These bars do not serve alcohol but instead serve a wide range of nonalcoholic beverages, ranging from nonalcoholic beers, dealcoholized wines, and mocktails meant to imitate alcoholic beverages, or drinks that are just meant to taste good. While not everyone at a sober bar is sober, they are a great place to meet people who are exploring sobriety or are at least open to socializing without alcohol.

☐ **Day breaker:** This is a morning sober dance party that happens in cities all over the United States. Sometimes they start out with a yoga or movement class before bringing out a DJ or live instruments. The party takes places in the morning to encourage sobriety and spirituality. This is a great way to meet new people who like to socialize without alcohol, and it can also be a way to dance if the nightclubs are no longer for you.

☐ **Volunteer opportunities:** What causes are you passionate about? For example, if you love animals, you may find friends while volunteering at a local animal shelter. If you care about children, volunteer at a local pediatric hospital where you can meet other likeminded people. Protests can also be a great way to meet people who care about the same issue as you. See if there are local organizations you can get involved with in your area.

☐ **12-step and/or recovery-based meetings** (AA, NA, Al-Anon, SMART, Yoga of 12 Step Recovery, Refuge Recovery): You can find these meetings in person or online, and many (especially 12-step groups) encourage a community of "fellowshipping," which involves socializing as a group before or after the meeting. You can find different types of meetings based on your interests, gender, or age.

☐ **Tap into your current network:** Think about the people you already know. Do you know any neighbors, acquaintances, or friends of friends? Is there anyone you would like to get to know better? Maybe you are already part of a club, meeting, or organization where there is someone you would like to know better. Ask them to get coffee sometime. Write down a list of at least 10 people you know who you would be open to connecting with on a deeper level. You don't even have to know their names—maybe it is a person who frequents your local coffee shop!

Finding Friends Online

☐ **Meetup.com** is a great website where you can search by activities (online or in person), join a club, or start your own. It allows you to find different clubs that are already formed or join local events in your area.

☐ **Nextdoor** is a great app that connects you with your neighbors. Your neighborhood may already be on Nextdoor. You simply sign up with your address and can chat with your neighbors and connect with local groups. It is a great way to get to know people in your area with less pressure than knocking on their door.

☐ Use **Instagram or other social media**. Join groups and follow pages and hashtags with similar interests—there are lots of sober groups and pages—and strike up a conversation with someone you respect. See if they are interested in grabbing coffee.

☐ Use a **friend-finding app**, like Atleto, Bumble BFF, Cliq, FriendMatch, Peanut, Meet My Dog, RealU, Skout, or Yubo. These are like dating apps but for friendship, some of which are based on interest. For example, Peanut is an app for moms to connect, Meet My Dog is for dog lovers, and RealU and Skout help you meet people around the globe. Find the one that sounds most appealing to you and try it out.

8

Sober Dating

Sober dating is like sober socializing on steroids. Not only do clients have to meet a new person and talk to them about the personal details of their lives, but there is also the possibility of sexual intimacy. And that person is likely to recommend that your client go out for a drink, which puts their drinking (or lack thereof) front and center. However, the beauty of sober dating is that clients can see the other person for who they are much more clearly without the haze of alcohol clouding their vision. It may be more uncomfortable, especially in the beginning when clients are getting used to sober socializing, but overall people who don't drink alcohol on dates are able to save a lot of time and energy because they can tell if someone is a match for them early on.

In fact, clients can learn a lot about someone simply by how that person reacts to them when they say that they don't drink. This may happen before your client even meets up in person. For example, some clients choose to put this information on their online dating profile, which can help weed out inopportune candidates from the get-go (more on this later in the chapter). Clients also have an opportunity to disclose their sober status if the other person suggests grabbing a drink on the first date (which, let's face it, is the suggestion for 99 percent of first dates).

Even if clients don't share about their sobriety beforehand, they can do so early on during the date, such as when the waiter is taking their drink order. If the other person makes fun of the client, tries to pressure them into drinking, calls them a derogatory name, or becomes defensive about their own drinking, these are all red flags that the client gets to discover about them *early*. On the other hand, if the other person is unbothered, curious, understanding, or—dare I say—respectful of your client's decision to not drink, these are undoubtedly green flags that your client also gets to discover very quickly.

> **Quick tip:** The first 15 minutes of a date (or any social gathering at a restaurant or bar) are the most difficult. It is during those first 15 minutes that many people on dates eagerly order a drink, which can cause sober clients to feel awkward, especially when the other person asks why the client isn't drinking. Here is where you want to encourage clients to draw on the list of responses to the dreaded "why" question from the last chapter. Remind clients that once the other person settles in, the energy shifts and they are much less likely to care if the client is drinking.

Another advantage to dating sober is that people tend to be more creative with date ideas. Most people do the same thing when it comes to going on a date—drinks or dinner—which can make dating feel like a drag after a while. It's no wonder that so many individuals cancel their dates at the last minute. But when a client is sober, they have a good excuse to suggest doing something different and interesting, whether it be ice skating, bowling, mini golfing, going to a museum, or even exploring a local park. These activity-based dates give clients something to focus on while they get to know the other person, which can help them get out of their head. If there is a pause in the conversation or a moment of silence, it doesn't feel as awkward because both parties are not staring at each other from across the table. These types of dates also give more opportunity for teasing, flirtation, and casual physical touch compared to the standard date.

Perhaps the biggest advantage to sober dating is that clients are more likely to stick to their values and not do something they regret. When people drink, the rational, decision-making part of the brain goes offline, preventing them from weighing how their behaviors will impact their future goals. As a result, they may do or say things they never would have otherwise had they not been drinking. In contrast, clients who are sober will be able to date more confidently knowing that they are living a life that is in alignment with what they want, need, and value in a relationship. Many clients see getting sober as a drawback when it comes to dating, so if you can help them see it as a positive, they may feel more optimistic and excited about the process.

Dating Inventory

Before you start dating without alcohol, it can be helpful to take stock of your past dating history. Use this worksheet to gain a deeper understanding into how alcohol played a role in your past romantic relationships or dating life and how your fears may be holding you back.

1. How much of a role did alcohol play in your past or current relationship? For example, did you and your partner often drink together? Did alcohol play a role in fights? Did drinking ever lead you to say or do things that you regretted or that harmed your relationship?

_____

_____

_____

_____

2. How much of a role did alcohol play in your past dating life? For example, are you someone who previously would never have considered going on a date without a drink? Did you ever "pregame" before your dates? Did you judge your dates by how much or little they drank? Did drinking ever lead you to make decisions on a date that you later regretted?

_____

_____

_____

_____

3. What are your biggest fears about dating sober?

_____

_____

_____

_____

4. What are some advantages you can think of to being sober when going on a date?

_____

_____

_____

_____

How to Date Sober

Like all things in sobriety, sober dating may be more difficult at first, but it will lead you to find a more genuine connection with someone. To help you navigate sober dating, look through the following checklist, which provides you with suggestions for dates that don't involve alcohol. Put a check mark by any activities that you'd be willing to try as you navigate sober dating.

- ☐ Go out for dessert
- ☐ Grab coffee
- ☐ Go ice skating
- ☐ Go bowling
- ☐ See a comedy show
- ☐ Go to a concert or live music performance
- ☐ Eat at a BYOB restaurant
- ☐ Attend a workout class
- ☐ Go for a hike
- ☐ Volunteer
- ☐ Go to a farmer's or flea market
- ☐ Visit an amusement park

- ☐ Go to a sports game
- ☐ Go mini golfing or to an arcade
- ☐ Go axe throwing
- ☐ Play ping pong
- ☐ Go to a trivia night
- ☐ Take a class (e.g., art, cooking, crafting)
- ☐ Visit a museum
- ☐ Go rock climbing
- ☐ Have a game night
- ☐ Go out dancing
- ☐ Have a picnic
- ☐ Take a walk
- ☐ Go to the beach

In addition, consider the following helpful responses that you can use when someone asks you out for a drink:

- ☐ "I'd love to, but I'm actually not drinking right now. How about we grab ice cream instead?"
- ☐ "That sounds great. I'm taking a break from drinking right now, but I know of a bar or restaurant that has great mocktails."
- ☐ "Sure, how about we grab coffee?"
- ☐ "I actually don't drink, but I would love to go grab an appetizer with you."
- ☐ "I'm taking a break from drinking, but I have been dying to go to this museum, exhibit, restaurant, etc."
- ☐ "I'd love to. I'm actually sober but am always down for a good mocktail."

Modern dating culture glorifies drinking as a way for clients to "loosen up" and feel more comfortable. While alcohol does reduce inhibitions, inhibitions also serve a purpose. An inhibition is a conscious or unconscious feeling or thought that holds us back from doing something. Our inhibitions keep us safe. They say, *I can't quite put my finger on it, but I'm getting a weird vibe from that person* or *Yes, I feel really comfortable with this person, but I don't feel ready to share that or do that.* Instincts motivate clients to set boundaries in their relationships and remind them of the long-term consequences of behaving in certain ways. Once clients realize this, it may be easier than they think to trade the initial discomfort of not drinking for actions that will get them closer to the life they want.

When Should Clients Start Dating?

Regardless of the advantages of sober dating, it is still stressful, which can be triggering for clients in early recovery. Furthermore, they may go out on some dates where the other person is actively drinking around them, which puts them at even greater risk for relapse. Other clients may "addiction switch" by jumping into a new relationship right away and allowing that person to consume their whole life. This is especially true in the case of clients who struggle with codependency; they essentially trade the time spent drinking and channel it into spending all their time with this new partner.

While codependency might seem like a preferable substitute to drinking, it can easily cause clients to relapse if the relationship ends, and this is likely to happen since most codependent relationships are unhealthy from the beginning. They are based in lust and mutual obsession instead of common values, trust, and respect. Even if the relationship does not culminate in a breakup, clients still miss out on building the important skills needed for long-term recovery, such as emotion regulation, healthy communication, and self-care.

For all these reasons, I recommend clients who are single wait until they are at least three to six months into recovery (and not experiencing regular cravings) before they begin dating. Some programs, such as AA, even recommend that clients not date until they have a full year of sobriety under their belt. As a clinician, you can learn about their dating patterns and relationship history to determine whether it would be beneficial for them to take a longer break before dating. In my experience, if clients are overly excited to date, or become protective or defensive about their dating history, this may be a sign that they should wait longer than three to six months. Unlike sober socializing, which is an important part of recovery, clients do not *need* to date in order to stop drinking.

Signs a Client May Need a Longer Break from Dating

- They have history of unhealthy romantic partnerships.
- They struggle with codependency (whether with family, friends, or significant others).
- They tend to jump from relationship to relationship and have not spent much time single.
- They seek out attention on dating apps as a form of validation.
- They have a moderate to severe alcohol use disorder.

Sober Online Dating

Dating apps are the most popular way to find potential love interests these days, so chances are that your clients will be using these apps to meet people. When a client is sober, they will need to decide whether they want to disclose their drinking status on their profile. Many apps have the option to indicate how much someone drinks, or clients can simply add this information to their bio. There are both pros and cons to disclosing this information. The pro is that clients will likely not have to engage in an entire conversation about their drinking status before going on a date. It is clearly indicated on their profile, so if the other person is paying attention, they hopefully will not suggest meeting at a bar. Another advantage is that it will weed out anyone who parties excessively or is disrespectful of the client's decision to remain sober. This can help counter the temptation that clients may have to hide their sobriety or convince themselves that they are okay with dating someone whose entire social life revolves around drinking. By disclosing their sober status on their profile, clients are less likely to match with these individuals in the first place.

Of course, a potential con of disclosing their sober status on their profile is that clients will get fewer matches. They may even receive snide or rude messages. When this happens, it can be helpful to remind clients that meeting people online is so difficult because each party is taking in only a few shreds of information about the other person, and the brain is filling in any remaining gaps to create an entire narrative. They do not actually know each other. However, it can still be painful if a client feels as though their worst fears about dating are coming true. In these cases, it may be helpful if the client takes a break from online dating. They can also investigate sober dating apps such as Loosid, Clean and Sober Love, MeetMindful, or Sober Singles Date.

In addition, explain to clients that one of the most common reasons people are not successful with online dating is not due to a lack of online matches; it is due to a lack of high-quality in-person meetups. Many people on dating apps are not seriously looking to date and are instead looking for validation. As a result, clients can fall into the trap of chatting with someone on the app or via text message for weeks or months but never meeting in person. This is when it is important to remind clients that the purpose of online dating is to help them meet someone. It is not to provide them with a pen pal or online partner.

Dating apps can also get very overwhelming if a client is trying to field conversations with multiple individuals without having met any in person. Yes, they can learn important information about someone through the app, but they cannot truly learn if they share the same values and would be compatible in a relationship if they never meet in person. When clients are juggling several romantic interests online, it can also lead to the crash-and-burn cycle, where clients become very motivated to date, sign up for tons of dating apps, and initiate several conversations, only to get overwhelmed by how it takes over their life. They then delete all the apps and take a break from dating, only to panic about being single and restart the cycle once again. To combat this, I typically recommend that clients only use a maximum of two apps at a time and be in conversations with no more than five people at once.

Finally, just because a client quits drinking, does not mean they need to date someone who is sober as well. As I will explain in the next section, there are positives and negatives to dating someone who is in recovery as well. Instead, encourage clients to focus on dating people who have a healthy relationship

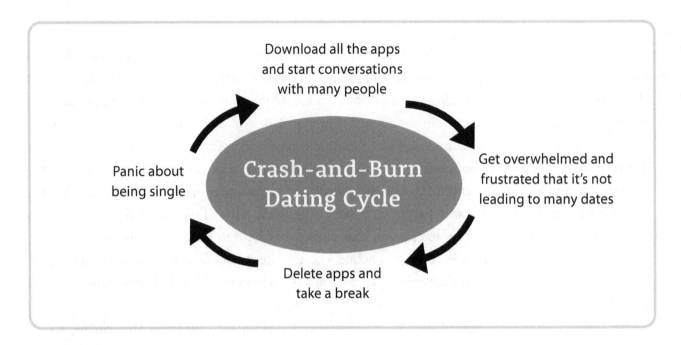

with alcohol. If their date only wants to go to a bar, this is a red flag. If they go out of their way to secure a drink at a miniature golf course, this is a red flag as well. If they tell the client, "Wow I can't believe you stopped drinking, I could never go on a date without a drink! What do you even do for fun?" it is likely they do not have a healthy relationship with alcohol.

While some clients may not mind dating a heavy drinker—I have even had clients say they prefer people like this—if their partner's main hobby is drinking, it is going to be difficult to spend quality time together. In addition, although newly sober clients may still think the idea of drinking is fun and don't mind if their date gets drunk, this will eventually get old. The next worksheet will give clients an idea of some red and green flags for assessing someone's relationship with alcohol.

Red and Green Flags

If you have changed your relationship with alcohol or quit drinking completely, it is likely going to impact how you date. This does not mean you cannot date someone who drinks, but it may change your interest in dating someone whose only hobby is bar hopping. It can also be triggering if you start spending a lot of time with someone who is drunk all the time. However, it can be difficult to assess if someone has a healthy relationship with alcohol, so use this worksheet to check for potential green or red flags. Keep in mind, these are not definitive. Green flags are a positive sign, while red flags are a warning light. Only you get to decide whether you feel comfortable with the red flags or if it is not worth meeting up with them again.

Green Flags

☐ They don't make a big deal of the fact that you don't drink.

☐ They seem to respect your choice to not drink.

☐ They suggest a new date idea when they learn you don't drink.

☐ They seem genuinely curious and interested about your alcohol-free life.

☐ They know a friend, family member, or someone who does not drink, and they respect that person.

☐ _____

Red Flags

☐ They make a joke about how they could never be sober.

☐ They ask, "Well, then what do you do for fun?!"

☐ They are not willing to go on a date without alcohol.

☐ On the date, they go out of their way to get a drink.

☐ They have more than three drinks on the date.

☐ _____

After going out with this person or briefly chatting with them online, do you feel like you want to spend more time with them? Why or why not?

_____

_____

_____

If a client is sober curious and exploring their relationship with alcohol more loosely, it may not be authentic for them to indicate that they do not drink alcohol on their profile. It may also be less important for them to date someone who has a healthy relationship with alcohol, especially if the client is still part of the drinking culture and is able to moderate their drinking. However, if a client truly has had a history of problematic or out-of-control drinking, being around a heavy drinker can have a negative impact. Either way, it is important to explore how your client would feel and react if they dated someone whose main hobby is alcohol.

What If Your Client's Partner Drinks?

If clients are in a relationship with someone who drinks, they may want their partner to stop drinking so they can experience the magic of sobriety too. Your client may also start to notice how their partner uses alcohol to numb out, de-stress, or deal with their emotions. They may worry that their significant other drinks too much and want to point out all the ways that alcohol isn't truly helping them. It may be frustrating when clients wake up refreshed and ready to go on Sunday morning only for their partner to have a hangover and not want to leave the couch. And let's be honest, sober sex is great, but not when the other person is drunk.

Although many clients are tempted to coerce or convince their partner into sobriety, the absolute best chance that clients have of convincing their partner to quit drinking alongside them is to inspire them rather than try to force them to change. That's because humans naturally resist change. A relationship unit—consisting of two people or more—wants to maintain the status quo, so one person in the relationship is likely to push back on any type of change. I've had people beg me to help their significant other quit drinking, only for the client to push back when their newly sober partner starts setting boundaries that they don't like.

This doesn't mean that your client's relationship is doomed. It *does* mean that clients may need to help their partner understand that sobriety is something they are doing for themselves, and they are not trying to change their partner. It may also be helpful for clients to share how *their partner* will benefit from the client being sober. For example, the other person won't have to worry about the client's physical health, they may get into less drunken disagreements, and the client will no longer need someone to take care of them at three in the morning.

AA has a slogan that stresses attraction over promotion—meaning that recovery cannot be promoted; it is something people need to become attracted to themselves—and I couldn't agree more. Clients simply cannot force their partner into recovery. While this may feel like a bummer for many clients, it is important to remind them that every relationship has its challenges and compromises. Life is complicated, and being in a committed partnership is no exception. There will always be stressors, but it is possible to be in a relationship where one person drinks and the other does not. It's also worth pointing out that even folks in sober relationships encounter their fair share of stressors, whether it is navigating relapse, worrying about the other person slipping, or being overly dependent on each other to stay sober. No relationship is perfect. Clients get to decide what works for them.

Fears in a Relationship

Telling your significant other that you want to stop drinking can come with a lot of fear. While these fears are valid, sometimes what you imagine will happen is not realistic. If you can name these fears, it will be easier to work through them and determine the probability that they will come true. Answer the questions below to tame your fears. Remember, avoidance of anything tends to increase your anxiety over time.

1. The following are some common fears that people may experience when one person in the relationship decides to stop drinking. Put a check mark by any that you relate to:
   - ☐ What if I change and they don't like me or think I'm fun anymore?
   - ☐ What if I change and I realize I don't like them?
   - ☐ What if I outgrow them?
   - ☐ What if I discover I have nothing in common with my significant other?
   - ☐ What if I married my drinking buddy? What are we going to do if I quit drinking?
   - ☐ What if they aren't supportive and judge me?

2. What are your biggest fears about taking a break from alcohol if your significant other drinks? What is the worst-case scenario that you go to in your mind?

   _____

   _____

   _____

3. How likely is your worst-case scenario to happen? For example, has your partner been unsupportive of others who've cut back on drinking? Do they often pressure others to keep up and drink? Do you spend a significant amount of time together drinking? Are your partner's other relationships (e.g., with family, friends) also based on their communal drinking? Answering these questions can help you discover how your partner may react.

   _____

   _____

   _____

Dealing with Fallout

Unfortunately, worst-case scenarios do happen. Clients may discover that they've outgrown their partner or married their drinking buddy. Sometimes alcohol is the unspoken glue that holds a dysfunctional relationship together. Once clients start discovering these incompatibilities with their partner, they will need support in identifying if they want to walk away from the relationship or continue trying to make it work. Many clients will feel pressured to make an immediate decision. However, they do not need to decide right now. In fact, it can be helpful for them to take some time to think over what they want and need. Clients likely have many different conflicting emotions, and this makes sense. Just because some of their fears have been realized does not mean that feelings for their partner will vanish.

When navigating this difficult scenario, some clients may tell you that they wish they never got sober. They may long to return to the way things were. Of course, clients can make the choice to resume drinking if they so choose, but it is important to remind them that it is hard to unlearn what they have already discovered. Once a client realizes that their relationship has been based on alcohol, it may never feel the same again, even if they start drinking again. In addition, if the only thing that was keeping the relationship together was alcohol, there were likely other issues going on.

Just because a client feels grief, sadness, anger, or any number of emotions does not mean they are making the wrong choice. So often, clients feel torn because they expect themselves to not have any doubts about whether they are making the right decision. However, rarely in life are things all good or bad. Clients probably have a mixture of positive and negative memories when it comes to their significant other. Give them freedom to explore all the pros and cons of the relationship without encouraging them to stay or go. Instead, remind them that your only goal is to help them achieve their goals, regardless of what they want. The next worksheet will help clients evaluate if they want to stay in the relationship or leave.

When Fears Come True

Sometimes your worst fears come true in a relationship: Your partner is not supportive of your sobriety, you realize you don't have much in common without alcohol, and you no longer find their drunk antics amusing. This realization can be crushing. It can lead you to question if you should stay in the relationship or leave. This is a question only you can answer for yourself. However, by answering the questions here, you'll learn more about your relationship and determine whether there are other positive qualities you are overlooking or whether your relationship is perhaps no longer healthy.

1. What are the best parts of your relationship? For example, perhaps you work well together as parents or enjoy spending time together with your shared friend group.

   _____

   _____

   _____

   _____

2. What are the most difficult parts of your relationship? For example, perhaps you frequently get into nasty fights or struggle with a lack of physical intimacy.

   _____

   _____

   _____

   _____

3. Do you and your partner still enjoy doing activities together that don't involve drinking? If so, what types of hobbies or pursuits still bring you simultaneous pleasure? If not, are there any activities that you used to enjoy in the past that you can revisit?

   _____

   _____

_____

_____

4. Are you both able to communicate with each other when sober? If not, have you gone to therapy (either together or separately) or read any books to try to improve your communication skills?

_____

_____

_____

_____

5. What values do you have in common? For example, perhaps you both value honesty, family, travel, achievement, and so on. Have these values changed since you stopped drinking? Have your partner's values changed over the course of your relationship?

_____

_____

_____

_____

6. Why did you initially start dating? What drew you to each other? What did you have in common? What made you fall in love? Does your partner still have any of those qualities today?

_____

_____

_____

_____

7. Do you think your partner has disordered drinking? If they do and are not willing to quit, is this something you are willing to accept?

_____

_____

_____

_____

8. Does your partner say or do things when intoxicated that put you or your family at risk? Do they act abusively? Is it a recurring pattern?

_____

_____

_____

_____

9. After answering these questions, check in with yourself and take a breath. How are you feeling? What connections or realizations did you make from completing this worksheet?

_____

_____

_____

_____

Boundary Negotiation

Even if clients are in a relationship where their partner is supportive or tolerant of their sobriety, they have a right to set boundaries. Sometimes this may require some negotiating so both parties can get their needs met. In working with clients to set boundaries, it is helpful for them to think about nonnegotiables versus preferences. In general, a nonnegotiable boundary is something that either interferes with a client's sobriety or interferes with the integrity of the client's relationship. For example, a client may ask their partner to partake in certain activities without them, such as going to a work party or socializing with their college buddies, because the client finds it too triggering.

A preference, on the other hand, is much more flexible. For example, a client may prefer that no alcohol be kept in the home, but if they live with a partner who still drinks, this may not be possible. In this case, it can take some compromising to come up with a solution that works for both parties. Maybe their partner can agree to only purchase smaller amounts of alcohol that they can consume that week so there isn't an excess left around the house. However, if the client feels that it will be a risk to their recovery, this may not be a compromise that they can make. The longer a client is in recovery, the more likely their boundaries around alcohol may change. Initially, they may feel very triggered in the presence of alcohol and need their partner to keep it out of the house, but as they get more comfortable in their recovery, this may not bother them.

In my experience, clients in recovery tend to miscategorize some of their needs as preferences when they are really nonnegotiables. For example, it is incredibly difficult to make a relationship work if a client's partner is not supportive of their sobriety. This is typically a nonnegotiable boundary. However, clients sometimes worry that they are being too harsh or controlling if they voice their needs. In turn, they may act like they are okay with certain behaviors, such as their partner drinking around them. This can lead to more serious fights later as the non-sober partner can feel as if the client set them up by "pretending" to tolerate these behaviors early on. It is important for clients to be honest about their nonnegotiable boundaries from the start.

As clients navigate boundaries with their partner, here are some helpful phrases they can consider for common issues that arise:

- "I know questioning my relationship with alcohol has come with some challenges for you, and I appreciate you sticking by me through it. I am noticing having alcohol in our fridge is hard for me, can we talk about this?

- "I really don't feel up for going out to a restaurant and seeing people drink after the week I've had. Can we order takeout instead?"

- "I really want to go with you to your work party, but I am feeling really triggered and don't want to drink too much. I know this is disappointing, but I cannot go tonight. I have to put myself first in this situation."

- "I am feeling a little overwhelmed thinking about meeting all your friends today. I want to go, and I also want to make sure I don't push myself too much. Can we come up with a plan of what to do if I need to duck out early?"

Boundary Negotiation

If you are in a relationship with someone who drinks, it is likely you will need to negotiate boundaries around alcohol. This is even more important if you live together because some of your boundaries (e.g., keeping alcohol outside of the home) may interfere with some of your partner's. Use this worksheet to help identify your nonnegotiable boundaries and preferences around alcohol.

The following is a list of common boundaries that people negotiate in sobriety. Indicate whether each example is a nonnegotiable for you (N) or a preference (P). If an item is not important to you or does not apply, just leave it blank. Feel free to add additional boundaries if applicable.

_____ Not keeping alcohol in your fridge or kitchen (where it is visible)

_____ Not keeping alcohol in your home at all (even if it is hidden)

_____ Creating a safe word so you can leave an event if triggered

_____ Not going to bars

_____ Not going to certain places that you used to drink, such as: _____

_____ Having your partner not drink alcohol around you

_____ Not having your partner drink during the week

_____ Having half of your date nights be alcohol free

_____ Having your partner not get drunk around you

_____ If you split checks with your partner, not paying for your partner's alcohol when they drink

_____ Needing at least one evening alone for self-care

_____ Not attending certain events or gatherings if you are feeling triggered or overwhelmed

_____ A willingness to go to therapy if the relationship hits roadblocks

_____ Other: _____

_____ Other: _____

After thinking about your nonnegotiables versus your preferences, it is important to have an honest conversation with your partner about what you need in your relationship. Commit to having a conversation sometime this week. Giving yourself a deadline can help keep you accountable. Remember, too, that boundaries can change and evolve as needed. These are not set in stone, so this is a conversation that you will likely need to revisit in the future as you get further into your recovery.

9

Sober Sex and Pleasure

When most of us think about sex, we imagine music, mood lighting, and a drink to take the edge off. If dating without alcohol is scary, sober sex can seem impossible. Without alcohol, sex becomes a very intimate act that requires clients to be fully present with themselves and others. However, if a client already struggles to be present in their own body and with their own emotions, adding another human to that equation makes it even more difficult.

Many clients are never given the opportunity to question their relationship with sex and self-pleasure. They learn about sex from their caregivers, the media, and their friends. Maybe their parents read them books about sex or had "the talk." Maybe they didn't and that spoke volumes. Depending on a client's gender identity and sexual orientation, they may also have been shamed for whom they loved, or told that they would lose their value if they had sex before marriage. When clients internalize these beliefs, it makes it more difficult for them to feel comfortable and present during sex. They may feel guilty or ashamed about what turns them on, how their body looks, or what they find pleasurable. Women, trans and nonbinary folks, and other members of the LGBTQ+ community, in particular, are likely to have more shame around sex, pleasure, and their body.

However, even if a client is not a member of a marginalized community, it is rare for individuals, especially in the United States, to grow up in a sex-positive environment. Human sexuality is still viewed as a taboo topic. There is not comprehensive sex education in most schools across the country, especially in the South. In fact, sex education is often more about abstinence (which we know is ineffective at preventing STIs and teen pregnancy) than anything else. Religion also has a huge influence on our society, and there are many puritanical belief systems that position sex as an animalistic act that reflects a lack of self-control. Christianity, which is by far the most popular religion in the United States, often goes further. Many sects believe that premarital sex, masturbation, and birth control are all sins. In these religious sects, clients are often taught that their worth is tied to their virginity and that having sex before marriage will make them undesirable and dirty.

Even if a client is not raised in a religious household, purity culture filters down these messages into the information people consume in the mainstream media. In turn, alcohol becomes a mechanism that clients can use to numb themselves from these underlying beliefs they have internalized. Therefore, before clients dive into having sober sex, it's important to understand their sexual history and beliefs. This will allow them to understand why sober sex can be such a hurdle to overcome and how they can work through their fears, anxieties, and insecurities without turning to alcohol.

Sexual Inventory

Your early sexual experiences and those of your friends have a bigger impact on your relationship with sex than you might realize. They lay the foundation for your beliefs and values about sex and your body. In addition, what was modeled to you growing up—including the messages you received from your caregivers, the media, and society as a whole—informs your underlying thoughts about sexual pleasure and satisfaction. Use these questions to examine the messages you received about sex, including how they have impacted your sexuality today.

1. How did you first learn about sex? For example, did anyone give you "the talk"? Did you hear about it from classmates? Movies? Television? Did you discover porn at a young age?

_____

_____

_____

_____

2. What beliefs does your family have about sex that may have influenced your own attitudes toward it? For example, did your family talk openly about sex? How did they react to sex being portrayed in the media? What messages did you receive about how you dressed and its connection to sex? Were you raised in a religion that created shame about sex?

_____

_____

_____

_____

3. What do you think about when you hear the word *pleasure*?

_____

_____

_____

4. How did you first learn about masturbation and self-pleasure? How has this shaped your relationship with it?

_____

_____

_____

_____

5. What is the best or most positive sexual experience you've ever had? What made it so positive? Who was there? What happened? How did you feel?

_____

_____

_____

_____

6. What is the worst or most unpleasant sexual experience you've ever had? What made it so unpleasant? Who was there? What happened? How did you feel?

_____

_____

_____

_____

7. What gives you sexual pleasure or satisfaction that you don't ask for when having sex? What does *not* give you pleasure or satisfaction that you don't speak up about?

_____

_____

_____

_____

8. What are your biggest fears about having sex while sober?

_____

_____

_____

_____

Is Alcohol an Aphrodisiac?

Many people are sold on the idea that alcohol is an aphrodisiac that makes them feel sexy. But if you dig into what is *actually* happening when people drink, the truth is that alcohol just shuts off the part of the brain that makes people feel self-conscious. When people are drunk, they're not actually more attractive, funnier, or better in bed; they just *feel* more confident because they aren't as concerned about how others are perceiving them. However, being sloppy isn't sexy. Being on the verge of puking isn't sexy. Slurring words isn't sexy. And the belief that clients will find other people more attractive when drinking (due to the effects of having "beer goggles") is a myth that has been discredited.[37] This is an important distinction because, for many clients, alcohol is so intertwined with sex and dating that it feels impossible to get into the mood without it.

Although many clients also believe they are more adventurous in bed when under the influence of alcohol—and thus more confident in knowing what they want—the reality is that their inhibitions are just lowered. While this can lead to a wider range of experiences, it's not actually helping clients get in touch with their own desires. It also means they are more likely to say yes to something that they would otherwise not consent to when sober. And if they have a partner, their sexual intimacy and comfort with each other is not going to increase if clients can only engage in or talk about certain sexual acts and desires when they are under the influence.

Intoxicated Sex Pros	Intoxicated Sex Cons
■ Reduces self-consciousness so clients feel more confident	■ Makes consent more blurry
■ Reduces inhibitions and fear so clients may be more willing to try new things	■ More difficult to orgasm/climax
■ Can initially increase arousal	■ More difficult to become aroused (e.g., men getting hard and women being lubricated)
	■ Client may say or do things they regret
	■ Can be sloppy
	■ Harder for clients to know what they want or need during sex
	■ Less pleasure and reduced orgasm intensity
	■ Reduced inhibitions may lead clients to say yes to things they aren't comfortable with
	■ More likely to engage in risky behavior (e.g., not using protection)
	■ Impedes true intimacy
	■ Makes clients less likely to discover what they actually like sexually

Alcohol also doesn't make sex *feel better*. At all. Alcohol literally dulls the nerve endings that allow us to experience sensation, which results in sex feeling less pleasurable. In men, alcohol also makes it more difficult to get an erection, while for women, it interferes with lubrication. It makes it difficult for women to have orgasms as well, with those who do climax experiencing less intense sensations.[38]

The effects of alcohol on sex don't just include the act of intercourse itself. Alcohol dulls the sensation of foreplay and all the intimacy that can lead up to intercourse. Most clients know the experience of being aroused simply by someone stroking the side of their face or holding their hand. They might recall getting goosebumps when someone gently whispered into their ear. Or they might have experienced intense butterflies when someone leaned in for a kiss. These are all experiences that alcohol completely dulls the sensations of. Therefore, while alcohol may help clients feel less nervous on a first date, it also prevents them from experiencing the excited butterflies of a first kiss. In our hyperactive world of social media and technology, these tiny moments and sensations are more important than ever because it is easy to forget that our real lives exist off the internet. There is an entire world to discover beyond our screens.

Objectification and Body Image

When women in particular start engaging in sober sex, one of the most common things that they struggle with is their body image. While anyone can have difficulty becoming aroused if they feel insecure about their body, women often struggle with this the most because society objectifies women far more than men. We see this in advertisements, where women's body parts are often showcased in isolation from the rest of the body, or where a woman herself is transformed into a literal object, like a beer can or a car. Due to this type messaging, it is no surprise that from an early age, women come to view themselves as an object to be admired as opposed to a human being. This results in women constantly monitoring their bodies and imagining how they look from an outside perspective. For example, they may tug on their clothes to make sure they are laying flat (out of fear that someone may perceive them as heavier), check how their body looks in every mirror or window, or imagine what someone else may think of their body at any given time, even if they are alone.

This is compounded by the conflicting messages that women have about their bodies. They are told that they need to be sexy but also leave something to the imagination. They are told to be thin but also have breasts and a butt. Advertisements have always objectified women, but things have gotten far worse as technology has advanced. Photo editing software is so normal that everyday individuals can download an app to change how they look in photos. It is common to see images of women whose heads are larger than their pelvis, which is an anatomical impossibility. Social media is only making this problem worse. With filters, nobody shows up online authentically anymore.

Self-objectification not only takes up a huge amount of energy, but it also makes it difficult for individuals to become aroused and reach climax. For example, let's say a client's partner starts kissing or caressing her. The client starts to feel a little bit aroused, and as they both continue kissing, the client's partner touches her arm. The client thinks, *Gross, he touched my fat!* She tries to snap out of it and come back to the moment, but the sensation of her skin on her partner's skin makes her self-conscious. Her partner then comments on how large her breasts are, which causes the client to think, *Have I gained weight? I haven't been eating anything different the past few months. Maybe I need to start exercising more!* All of these thoughts can make it difficult for a client to continue being intimate because they are mentally surveying every inch of their body and trying to determine how it looks.

Alcohol becomes a way that clients can numb these distracting messages during sex because when they are intoxicated, they feel less self-conscious about their body and are less fixated on how they look. Since alcohol lowers inhibitions, clients can also more easily verbalize what turns them on, especially if they have internalized the belief that they are a "slut" or "gross" for enjoying sex or having a certain fetish. However, alcohol is only a short-term solution for a client's shame around their body and sex. Over the long term, it prevents them from having to do the real work to heal their body image and accept their sexual desires.

Healing Body Image Concerns

As a clinician, there are a few ways to support a client in improving their body image. The first is to stop focusing on the client's size and weight. One of the biggest pitfalls you can make as a clinician is to assume that if a client achieves their weight loss goal, their body image issues will be solved. Weight loss is usually just a temporary fix to a deeper issue. Most individuals who lose weight still don't feel comfortable in their body because weight is often a scapegoat for deeper mental health issues. The inevitable truth is that the client will likely always feel like they don't not measure up in some way. In addition, the ideal body type is literally impossible to achieve; there will always be someone else who is more attractive, not to mention that the definition of attractiveness is an ever-moving target.

Therefore, you want to support your client in accepting their body in its current form. You can do so by asking them questions like "If you knew your body would never change, what would you wear? What would you do? How would you live your life differently? How would you take care of yourself differently?" Then encourage your client to start taking action by doing just that, even if their mindset has not changed yet. Often, individuals must act first—before they are ready—and their mind will slowly follow.

To counteract negative body image messaging, it's also important to encourage your client to diversify their social media feed. If clients are not mindful, they may only be exposing themselves to thin, white, cisgender, heteronormative, able-bodied individuals who have Eurocentric beauty features. Instead, suggest that they follow different types of people in all different bodies: Black and Brown folks, fat folks, people with disabilities, LGBTQ+ folks, older individuals, and people with different skin textures (e.g., acne, scars, wrinkles, and cellulite). In real life, there are different types of people, with different types of bodies—we just often do not see enough of them because of the media we consume. Clients may also follow many individuals who promote weight loss, diet products, clean eating, and unhealthy exercise habits. Have them unfollow anyone who does not make them feel good about themselves or pushes an unhealthy obsession with appearance.

Another way to support clients in healing their body image is to focus on body neutrality instead of body love. It can be easy to champion that your client should love their body, but this can be too lofty of a goal if a client is coming from a place of body hate or shame. It can make them feel like something is wrong with them if they are unable to love their body. Know that your clients do not need to love their body in order to recover from body image issues. Instead, aim for body neutrality. This means that clients don't have to love how their body looks, but they can respect it. They can appreciate everything that their body does for them. This work will be more difficult for clients in a fat body because of the stigma and fatphobia that exists in our society. Regardless of the amount of body acceptance they cultivate, clients who are fat are more likely to face mistreatment at the doctor's office, online, and in public spaces. For many of these clients, achieving body neutrality will involve allowing them the time and space to grieve the body they wish they had before they can accept the body they have.

> **Quick Tip:** If you are a thin provider, it can be important to acknowledge your privilege in avoiding barriers that a client in a larger body will have to face. You can say something like "I know it may be uncomfortable to hear me, someone in a smaller body, discuss body image and body neutrality. Would you like to talk about this?" If this is a central issue that a client is dealing with, you may need to engage in case consultation. (If possible, seek out experts who are people of color and exist in large bodies, as they have firsthand experience of fatphobia and oppression.) You may also refer your client to a therapist who specializes in body image work and who is in a body similar to your client's.

Finally, since many clients use alcohol to escape the discomfort of being in their body, it is important to teach them mindfulness skills that allow them to be present in their body. If they have a history of trauma, this is even more important, though you will need to provide them with grounding skills first to create a sense of safety in their body. To introduce mindfulness to your clients, encourage them to pay close attention to how their body feels throughout the day, such as when they are doing chores, walking, stretching, or sitting outside. See if they can also attune to moments of pleasure in their body. This does not just involve experiences of sexual pleasure, but anything that creates a positive sensation in their body. For example, they can take a shower and notice how the warm water feels on their skin, engage in a gentle self-massage, stretch their muscles, brush their hair, or do anything that feels good. Women and marginalized individuals are often told their pleasure is not important, so this work is critical.

Ideas for Improving Body Image and Experiencing Pleasure

Negative body image is one of the biggest barriers for individuals to have a healthy sex life. It prevents you from being present in your body during intimacy, which can reduce pleasure and your ability to orgasm. Although many individuals drink as a way to cope with their insecurities, alcohol is a temporary bandage that will not solve body image or intimacy issues. Instead, try implementing some of the suggestions on this list into your life.

1. **Aim for body neutrality** by focusing on the things your body allows you to do instead of on how it looks. You don't need to love your body to appreciate it or take care of it. What are 10 things that you appreciate about your body? What does it do for you?

   _____

   _____

   _____

2. **Stop waiting for your body to change.** Buy clothes that fit your body now. You can shop at thrift stores or see if people can donate clothes to you if you cannot afford new ones. Your body deserves to be taken care of now, as it is. Accepting your body doesn't mean that you approve of it or even like it; it means you stop fighting reality and start living in what *is*. How would you show up if you knew your body would not change? What would you do differently?

   _____

   _____

   _____

   What is one thing you can do to take care of your body as it is today?

   _____

   _____

   _____

3. **Expose yourself to different types of people and bodies.** Follow people on social media who look different from what is commonly portrayed online (i.e., white, cis, hetero, thin folks). Follow Black and Brown folks, fat folks, people with disabilities, LGBTQ+ folks, people wearing hijabs, or people wearing just their underwear. Normalize seeing different skin textures, acne, scars, wrinkles, and cellulite. Let yourself view all different types of bodies. What is it like to see people in different body types who look different from you or who diverge from what is normally shown in the media?

_____

_____

_____

4. **Practice mindfully being in your body.** You can do this by engaging in gentle movement (walking, stretching, yoga), doing an activity that requires being in your body (washing dishes, cleaning, organizing), or engaging in another task that elicits pleasant sensations, like taking a bath or shower, massage, body work, or acupuncture. Spend 10 minutes today practicing mindfulness in your body. What was the experience like for you? What did you notice?

_____

_____

_____

5. **Practice experiencing pleasure in your body.** This could be through sex, intimacy with another person, masturbation, or self-pleasure. If that feels like too much, explore ways you can experience pleasure in your body that are not sexual. For example, take a warm bath, brush your hair, do a self-massage, or practice gua sha. What is one way you can practice seeking pleasure in your body?

_____

_____

_____

For 10 minutes, engage in one of these pleasurable activities. What was the experience like for you? Did any emotions come up?

_____

_____

_____

Accelerators and Brakes

In *Come as You Are,* Emily Nagoski talks about the dual control model of sexual response, which explains how and why individuals get turned on and off. We have two models that work together: the sexual excitation system (SES), which is an "accelerator" of our sexual interest, and the sexual inhibition system (SIS), which is the "brake." According to Nagoski, "Just as the accelerator scans the environment for turn-ons, the brake scans for anything your brain interprets as a good reason not to be aroused right now—risk of STI transmission, unwanted pregnancy, social consequences, etc."[39]

In order to understand how easily someone can get aroused, we must determine how sensitive their brakes and accelerator are. For example, someone with a higher sex drive will have a very sensitive accelerator and a sluggish brake, meaning that many things can turn them on and few things can turn them off. In contrast, someone with a lower sex drive will have a sluggish accelerator and a very sensitive brake, so it takes a lot to turn them on and not much to turn them off. The accelerator and brake work independently, yet they both impact a person's sex drive. You can think of this like a car: The break and gas pedals are not connected—you can hit both without releasing the other—but if you hit them at the same time, they cancel each other out. The same is true for sexual brakes and accelerators. No matter how sensitive someone's accelerator is (i.e., how easily aroused they are), if something is also pressing on the brake, they are not going to get turned on. Therefore, arousal is a two-part process. One part involves hitting the accelerator and the other involves taking one's foot off the brake.

It probably won't come as a surprise that men tend to have more sensitive sexual accelerators, while women tend to have more sensitive brakes.[40] This happens for a few reasons. First, men are more likely to experience spontaneous desire, meaning that their desire for sex can show up out of the blue, regardless of the context. This is most often the type of eroticism that is portrayed in the media. Women, in contrast, are more likely to exhibit responsive desire, in which the desire for sex occurs in response to physical arousal. In other words, most women require some sort of physical stimulation to get in the mood. Many couples experience more spontaneous desire at the beginning of their relationship or during the "honeymoon phase," and then progress to responsive desire as the relationship progresses.

Second, women are also more likely than men to have sensitive brakes because they engage in self-objectification. They get caught up in their heads—always monitoring how their body looks or how they might be perceived by others—which can interfere with their ability to get aroused. Alcohol becomes a great way to manage this negative self-talk because it turns off the part of the brain that criticizes how we look. In addition, alcohol allows clients (and women in particular) to temporarily stop worrying if they will be slut-shamed later, since alcohol makes them forget about the potential repercussions of their actions. For clients who have a history of trauma and struggle to feel safe in their body, alcohol also numbs the part of the brain that sends them into a state of fight, flight, or freeze.

It's for this reason that the prospect of sober sex can be downright terrifying to many clients. Alcohol makes their sexual brakes less sensitive. It mutes their turn-offs, making it easier to get sexually aroused. However, to get in the mood, clients cannot just focus on what turns them on; they must also learn what turns them off. In fact, studies show that an overly responsive brake is the greatest predictor of sexual dysfunction in both genders.[41] Therefore, it is crucially important that clients learn how to manage their sexual brakes without numbing them. To do this, clients first need to learn what their accelerators and brakes are, as well as how sensitive their accelerator and brakes are, which is known as their sexual temperament.

Accelerator and Brakes

You can think of sexual arousal like the inner workings of a car. There are certain things that turn you on (like a car's accelerator) and certain things that turn you off (like the brakes). Contrary to popular belief, arousal does not just occur in response to physical touch. It can also be in response to certain sights, smells, thoughts, memories, and emotions. The same is true for turn-offs. While alcohol is touted as an aphrodisiac, it only makes you less sensitive to your turn-offs. This worksheet will help you better understand your accelerators and brakes so you can reduce the impact of your turn-offs without drinking.

Common Accelerators	Common Brakes
▪ Consuming erotic media	▪ Stress
▪ Seeing your partner do something they are good at or in a new context (e.g., at work)	▪ Lack of trust
	▪ History of sexual trauma
▪ Feeling desired by or connected to someone	▪ Fear of being caught (though this can also be an accelerator for some)
▪ Certain smells (e.g., their perfume or cologne)	▪ Body shame
	▪ Self-consciousness
▪ Engaging in foreplay	▪ Performance anxiety
▪ Engaging in sexual cosplay (i.e., when someone wears a certain uniform or outfit)	▪ Concerns about reputation or being used
	▪ Feeling pressured to have sex

Think of what activates your accelerator and what activates your brakes. Write them down here. If you have trouble thinking of ideas, remember back to some of your best and worst sexual experiences from earlier in the chapter. What did they have in common?

What Activates Your Sexual Accelerator?	What Activates Your Sexual Brakes?

Sexual Temperament Questionnaire

After you have discovered what your accelerators and brakes are, it is important to understand how sensitive they are. This is known as your sexual temperament. Becoming familiar with your sexual temperament is important because arousal is a two-part process: activating your accelerators and disabling your brakes. Even if you get turned on easily, if your brakes are over-active, this will still make it difficult for you to have sex. Most sexual dysfunction is caused by oversensitive brakes.

Answer the following questions to discover your sexual temperament. Use the following key to describe your experience:

0	1	2	3	4
Not at all like me	Not much like me	Somewhat like me	A lot like me	Exactly like me

Sexual Brakes

_____ 1. Unless things are "just right," it is difficult for me to become sexually aroused.

_____ 2. When I am sexually aroused, the slightest thing can turn me off.

_____ 3. I must trust a partner to become fully aroused.

_____ 4. If I am worried about taking too long to become aroused or to orgasm, this can interfere with my arousal.

_____ 5. Sometimes I feel so self-conscious during sex that I cannot become fully aroused.

Total brakes score: _____ (out of 20)

Sexual Accelerators

_____ 1. Often just how someone smells can be a turn-on.

_____ 2. Seeing my partner doing something that shows their talent or intelligence, or watching them interacting well with others, can make me very sexually aroused.

_____ 3. Having sex in a different setting than usual is a real turn-on for me.

_____ 4. When I think about someone who I find sexually attractive or when I fantasize about sex, I easily become sexually aroused.

_____ 5. Certain hormonal changes (e.g., my menstrual cycle) increase my sexual arousal.

_____ 6. I get very turned on when someone wants me sexually.

Total accelerator score: _____ (out of 24)

Scoring Key

How Sensitive Is Your Brake?	How Sensitive Is Your Accelerator?
Not Very Sensitive (Score of 0–6) When you are engaging in sex, you are not easily distracted or turned off. You do not describe yourself as sexually reserved; in fact, the bigger issue is having to hold yourself back because many circumstances can become sexual for you.	**Not Very Sensitive (Score of 0–7)** It takes deliberate effort and attention for you to get turned on. You do not have spontaneous desire. Consistency, such as planning out when you engage in sex and using toys that increase stimulation, may help increase your sex drive.
Middle of the Road (Score of 7–13) Your sexual brakes are somewhat sensitive. Whether they kick in is often a function of the environment and how you are feeling. If you are feeling stressed, anxious, or self-conscious, your brakes can kick in. New or risky situations may also activate your brakes.	**Middle of the Road (Score of 8–15)** Your sexual accelerator is somewhat sensitive, and whether it kicks in largely depends on the context. You are more easily turned on in romantic or sexy situations. Conversely, it may be hard to experience spontaneous desire, especially in situations that are not romantic.
Very Sensitive (Score of 14–20) Your brakes are very easily triggered. This means that you may get easily distracted during sex or that stressful situations turn you off. You probably need to completely trust your partner and not feel rushed. If you have a history of trauma, it is likely your brain is hypervigilant to protect you from danger.	**Very Sensitive (Score of 16–24)** You get turned on very easily. A wide range of environments or contexts can elicit arousal, even ones that aren't romantic or erotic. Exciting, risky, or new situations may be very stimulating for you. You may also use sex as a way to de-stress.

Were you surprised by your findings about your sexual temperament? Why or why not? How do you feel after learning this?

_____

_____

_____

_____

10

Relapse Prevention

Whether a client is interested in abstaining from alcohol completely or taking a few months off, it's important for them to come prepared with the right tools that prevent them from drinking and prepare them to deal with cravings. All cravings start with a trigger, whether clients are aware of it or not. Sometimes clients are aware of what their triggers are before they even enter the situation. For example, they may know that an upcoming family gathering will be stressful, which allows them to prepare for the event or decline the invitation. However, other triggers are more unexpected. Someone might offer a client a bottle of champagne because they got promoted, or a client might run into an old drinking buddy who offers to catch up. In either case, it is vitally important to help clients understand their triggers so they know how to manage them as they arise. This is the case whether a client wants to moderate their drinking or stop altogether.

There are four major types of triggers that are important to help your client prepare for: emotional, environmental, exposure, and temporal. *Emotional triggers* refer to certain emotions that activate the desire to drink. Almost all clients with a history of problematic drinking will have experiences of turning to alcohol to numb or regulate their emotions. However, it's important for clients to understand which emotions are most triggering to them. For some clients, it may be anger, while for others it is sadness or loneliness. When clients take a break from drinking, it can help them get clear about their emotional triggers and how to regulate their emotions without alcohol.

Environmental triggers refer to any physical or sensory cues in the client's surroundings that create a desire to drink. This can include being in a location where the client used to consume alcohol, like a bar or the office, or even a room in their house. It can also involve being exposed to any sights, smells, or sounds that remind the client of drinking. For example, a whiff of orange juice might remind clients of all the screwdrivers they used to consume, or a particular song might remind them of the late nights they used to spend out at the bar. Environmental triggers can also come in the form of people that the client wants to avoid, like a client's drinking buddy or ex-partner, who can elicit the desire to drink.

Exposure triggers include situations where the client encounters alcohol or sees someone else consuming alcohol, which results in the craving to drink. This could involve being around people who are drinking at a family gathering, watching someone whip out a flask at a meeting, being offered a drink on a plane, or finding a bottle of wine that they had forgotten was in their basement.

Temporal triggers refer to certain times of the day or year, or holidays, associated with the desire to drink. This could be as simple as the clock striking 5:00 p.m., a client wanting to celebrate their birthday by popping champagne, or longing for Grandma's eggnog at a holiday gathering.

Encourage your client to get curious about these four types of triggers. Over the next 14 days, have your client make a list of their emotional, environmental, exposure, and temporal triggers. Ideally, have them identify at least 10 triggers from each category. These don't need to be triggers that your client has personally experienced; they can involve situations that your client believes could be triggering. Once they have a good understanding of their triggers, have them make a plan to handle their top five triggers in each category.

Identify Your Triggers

One of the most important aspects of relapse prevention involves knowing what your triggers are so you can take care to avoid them when possible or manage them when they unexpectedly pop up. Over the next 14 days, make a list of your emotional, environmental, exposure, and temporal triggers. Identify your top five triggers and think about the action you will take to prevent yourself from drinking, including how you will remove yourself from the situation if need be and to whom you can reach out for support.

Emotional triggers are any emotions that make you want to drink, like anger, sadness, or loneliness. This can also include any events or experiences that are likely to result in these particular emotions. Make a list of at least 10 emotional triggers, then plan for how you will handle the top five triggers.

_____

_____

_____

Example: "If I feel lonely and want to drink, I will call a friend to feel more connected."

1. If _____ (the trigger),

   I will _____ (action you will take).

2. If _____ (the trigger),

   I will _____ (action you will take).

3. If _____ (the trigger),

   I will _____ (action you will take).

4. If _____ (the trigger),

   I will _____ (action you will take).

5. If _____ (the trigger),

   I will _____ (action you will take).

Environmental triggers refer to anything in your immediate surroundings that make you want to drink. This can include certain sights, smells, sounds, or even people. Make a list of at least 10 environmental triggers, then plan for how you will handle the top five triggers.

_____

_____

_____

_____

Example: "If I get a craving for a drink when I watch my spouse crack open a beer, I will make myself a mocktail."

1. If _____ (the trigger),

   I will _____ (action you will take).

2. If _____ (the trigger),

   I will _____ (action you will take).

3. If _____ (the trigger),

   I will _____ (action you will take).

4. If _____ (the trigger),

   I will _____ (action you will take).

5. If _____ (the trigger),

   I will _____ (action you will take).

Exposure triggers refer to situations where you are exposed to alcohol, whether you discover it in your house, are offered it, or see other people drinking on social media or in real life. Make a list of at least 10 exposure triggers, then plan for how you will handle the top five triggers. For exposure triggers, one of the most helpful things you can do is remove yourself from the situation if you are able.

_____

_____

_____

_____

Example: "If someone offers me a shot, I will say no and go to the bathroom to remove myself from the situation, take a break, and go home early if I need to."

1. If _____ (the trigger),

   I will _____ (action you will take).

2. If _____ (the trigger),

   I will _____ (action you will take).

3. If _____ (the trigger),

   I will _____ (action you will take).

4. If _____ (the trigger),

   I will _____ (action you will take).

5. If _____ (the trigger),

   I will _____ (action you will take).

Temporal triggers involve any holidays, special occasions, or times of the day where you want to drink. Make a list of at least 10 temporal triggers, then plan for how you will handle the top five triggers.

_____

_____

_____

_____

Example: "If I get a craving to drink on my birthday, I will organize a birthday outing with my friends that is at a BYOB."

1. If _____ (the trigger),

   I will _____ (action you will take).

2. If _____ (the trigger),

   I will _____ (action you will take).

3. If _____ (the trigger),

   I will _____ (action you will take).

4. If _____ (the trigger),

   I will _____ (action you will take).

5. If _____ (the trigger),

   I will _____ (action you will take).

Coping with Cravings

No matter how well clients prepare for their triggers, they will all experience a craving for alcohol at some point. This is not something that they can prevent, so they need to learn how to deal with the craving by "surfing" the urge. An average craving lasts only 20 minutes, so it is important to ride the wave and wait for it to subside. The first thing clients can do when they experience a craving is to acknowledge it. They simply allow any thoughts or cravings to come up without trying to suppress them. This is the opposite of what many clients instinctually do, which is to shame themselves for having a craving. They think to themselves, *I can't believe I want a drink! I just committed to taking a break. This is never going to work.* However, when clients think this way, it only makes things worse—it stresses them out and makes them want to seek an escape, likely with alcohol. Instead, remind clients that cravings are normal and that they can simply acknowledge the craving without getting caught up in it.

The second step in riding out the urge is to remind clients that they can experience an urge and not act on it. Although cravings are unpleasant and uncomfortable, they won't last forever. Like a wave, the urge will rise in intensity, gradually peak, and then subside. However, sitting with this discomfort can be difficult for many clients, as most have low distress tolerance and use alcohol to cope with uncomfortable feelings, social anxiety, or a history of trauma. In order to ride the wave and increase their distress tolerance, encourage clients to remind themselves that, with time, the urge will pass. They do not need to give into the urge for it to go away. In fact, giving into the urge will only feel better for a short period of time.

Instead, it can be helpful to encourage your clients to create a self-soothe kit. This is a bag of sensory items that they can use to soothe themselves during an intense craving, such as candles or essential oils, tea, candy or gum, a fidget toy, a smooth rock, or a list of their top 10 reasons for staying sober. However, if they are in a place with easy access to alcohol, one of the most helpful things they can do is leave the situation. Sometimes clients need to be reminded that they should not try to test themselves or do anything to make sobriety more difficult.

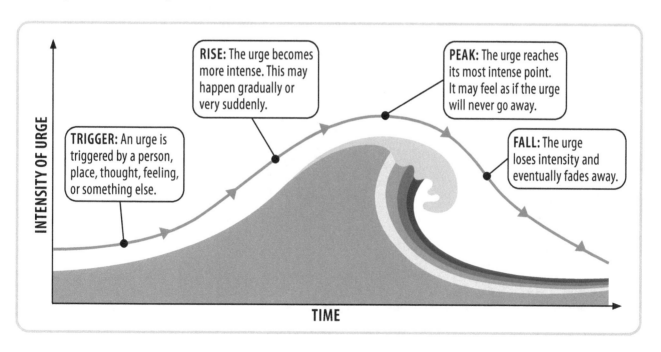

Finally, distraction is a useful third step that clients can use to keep their minds off the urge. This can include playing phone games, watching TV in bed, or scrolling on TikTok. It does not need to involve an enriching activity that is overly difficult or one that requires any motivation on the client's part. It should simply be something that the client wants to do that will help pass the time. What matters most is surviving the craving while staying sober. A craving is like an itch from a mosquito bite. The best thing clients can do in this situation is to acknowledge the craving, distract themselves, and leave it alone. When clients blame themselves, get angry, or act on the urge, it is as if they are scratching that mosquito bite. It may feel better temporarily, but it makes the itch worse later.

Urge Surfing

An urge is an intense craving or desire to act out of habit. To work through the urge to drink without giving into it, it is helpful to think of an urge like a wave. While you cannot stop the wave from coming, you can learn to ride it and use coping skills until the urge passes. An average craving only lasts 20 minutes. Use the following three steps to surf through your next craving.

1. **Acknowledge.** The first step of urge surfing is to notice that you are having a craving and acknowledge your thoughts and feelings. Be mindful not to beat yourself up for having a craving. Simply allow your thoughts and feelings related to this craving to arise without judgment—without trying to force them away. Write down any thoughts or feelings you are having here.

_____

_____

_____

_____

2. **Reassure yourself.** Just because you have an urge doesn't mean you have to act on it. Urges are normal and to be expected. They are not an indication of your commitment to your sobriety. You can survive being uncomfortable. Like a wave, the urge will eventually peak in intensity and then subside. Write down a phrase that reminds you of your ability to ride this wave—that you *can* do this no matter how uncomfortable it feels. Then repeat it to yourself.

_____

_____

_____

_____

3. **Distract yourself.** Do something that takes your full attention. Leave the situation if you are in the vicinity of alcohol or at risk for drinking. Go for a walk, play a game on your phone, take a shower, or watch a television show—just get your mind off the craving as much as you can. Your goal is to get through the craving right now. You can drink tomorrow if you still feel the urge. Write down a few different coping skills you can use to distract yourself, then pick one and practice doing it for 20 minutes.

_____

_____

_____

_____

What Is Your Client *Really* Craving?

When clients experience the urge to drink, they are actually experiencing a craving for what the drink represents. It is not necessarily the taste of alcohol that the client wants; it is the stress relief that accompanies it. Most clients can relate to the experience of letting out a sigh of relief at the end of the day when they crack open a beer. They feel that sense of relaxation before they even take a sip. That's because alcohol is such a powerful reinforcer that the brain feels some relief before the effects of alcohol even have a chance to set in. This reinforcing effect works with other associations that clients may have with alcohol too. For example, clients might have the urge to drink because they are craving connection, and they associate alcohol with being able to let loose and have fun. Or maybe they're craving a moment to themselves, and alcohol signifies that "alone time" in the evening when the kids are finally asleep and the client gets a moment of peace to themselves.

Therefore, it can be helpful for clients to ask themselves the following question after the intensity of the urge passes: *What am I really craving?* If clients can start to understand what they are really craving beyond the drink, they can take care of themselves more effectively. As Holly Whitaker says, sometimes what clients actually want is a "moment."[42] A moment where they can shut off their brain, pause, and maybe experience a little indulgence. Often, that moment can be created with a cup of tea, a mocktail, some time spent outside in the warm sunshine, or a delicious dessert.

Once clients have been abstinent for some time, cravings can serve as a warning sign that the client isn't meeting an underlying need. Similar to how a car's check engine light will turn on before something goes wrong, a craving lets clients know that something is off with their self-care that needs attention. A check engine light does not mean a car is broken, just like a craving for alcohol does not mean a client will relapse. It is an opportunity to get curious about what they may be feeling and tend to themselves.

What Are You Really Craving?

When you experience a craving for alcohol, the craving often isn't really about the drink itself; it's about what the drink represents. For example, you may associate alcohol with stress relief, connection, or fun—and *that's* what the true craving is about. In order to understand what your cravings mean to you, try the following exercise the next time you experience the urge to drink. Answer these questions after the most intense part of the craving has subsided and you have surfed the urge.

1. Think about your drinking rituals. Do you drink at a certain time of night? Do you drink on Mondays with friends while watching reality TV or sports games? Do you have a certain drinking ritual to end your week? Or any rituals that you do with friends, family, or your spouse? Write down any drinking rituals or habits that come to mind.

   _____

   _____

   _____

   _____

2. After identifying your drinking rituals and habits, do you see any patterns in how you are using alcohol? What are you really craving? Connection? A break? Stress relief? Fun? Spontaneity? Alone time? Indulgence? Think about the situations in which you use alcohol and dig deeper to think about what you are really craving in those moments.

   _____

   _____

   _____

   _____

3. Does drinking actually meet this need? Is there a better way you can fulfill this craving than drinking? For example, if you feel lonely, will drinking actually fulfill your need for social interaction? What will happen after the drink wears off? Do you have any fears about what will happen if you give up this ritual?

_____

_____

_____

_____

4. Play the tape through by imagining exactly what will happen if you drink again, from the moment you feel intoxicated, to the aftermath of what happens to you physically and emotionally. What will happen if you give into this craving? What will happen after you have that first drink? Will you be satisfied? Will you want another? How will you feel? How likely are you to keep drinking? Write down exactly what will happen, from beginning to end, if you drink right now. (You can either think about what has happened in your past or imagine what may happen if you have never relapsed before.)

_____

_____

_____

_____

Recovery Bank Account

One of my favorite tools for relapse prevention is to encourage clients to think of their recovery like a bank account. Certain activities, like going to therapy, getting enough rest, spending time in nature, and connecting with loved ones, are deposits that replenish their bank account. They support the client's sobriety and make it less likely that they will slip up and drink alcohol. However, other situations, like life transitions, breakups, and holiday parties, function as withdrawals from their bank account. Some withdrawals are not the client's choice or fault, as might happen when they encounter unexpected health issues, while other withdrawals are by choice, such as when a client spends time with an old drinking friend or goes on an all-inclusive vacation. Regardless, both types of withdrawals result in stress and make it more likely that clients will lapse into old patterns of behavior. Even withdrawals that are fun and enjoyable can be risky for a client's recovery, especially if they have not been sober for very long.

In addition, certain experiences or activities will "cost" more than others, depending on the situation and if it is the client's first time abstaining from alcohol. For example, when clients are newly sober, it may be difficult to just make it through a day without drinking. In these cases, even going to work or socializing with other people can function as withdrawals. Especially in the early stages of recovery, it is important that clients avoid any high-cost activities, since it's already taking a lot of day-to-day effort to keep their balance from going negative. As clients get further into their recovery, it will be easier to do things that are riskier, like going to an office party. However, it is important for clients to continue to be mindful of other withdrawals and to replenish their bank account on a regular basis with deposits that enhance their mental health. Some withdrawals are unexpected, like getting sick, so it is a good idea for clients to pad their balance in case of unforeseen stressors.

Recovery Bank Account

Your recovery is like a bank account. As you live your life, there will naturally be withdrawals from this account over time. Some will be small, such as getting stuck in traffic, while others will take a huge toll, such as getting fired. To counteract these withdrawals and not overdraft the account (i.e., relapse), you will need to make regular deposits into your recovery account. The challenge with deposits is that most of them only last a few hours or days, while withdrawals can last months or years. For example, getting fresh air might rejuvenate you for a few hours, going to therapy may make you feel better for a day or so, and going on a wellness retreat could last you a few weeks. Therefore, it is important to maintain daily self-care habits that replenish your bank account so you can account for unexpected or large withdrawals that you may not be able to control.

Fill in the empty spaces in the following chart to make note of your withdrawals and deposits. Next to each example, indicate how expensive the withdrawal or deposit is using a $, $$, or $$$ symbol. At the end, tabulate your answers so you can get an idea of how full your recovery account is and if you are at risk for a relapse:

Withdrawals	Deposits
$ Fairly stressful $$ Moderately stressful $$$ Extremely stressful	$ Rejuvenating (Reduces stress for a few hours) $$ Moderately rejuvenating (Reduces stress for a few days) $$$ Extremely rejuvenating (Reduces stress for a few weeks)
_____ Stress _____ Death of a loved one _____ Trauma _____ Dating _____ Moving _____ Going through a breakup (partner, friendship, or otherwise) _____ Childbirth	_____ Eating well _____ Getting enough sleep _____ Going to therapy _____ Reading _____ Getting fresh air _____ Taking medicine as prescribed _____ Practicing self-care _____ Moving your body

_____ Getting divorced	_____ Meditating
_____ Getting sick	_____ Doing body work
_____ Job changes	_____ Using coping skills
_____ Getting stuck in traffic	_____ Making time for hobbies
_____ Witnessing trauma and pain on the news	_____ Taking a mental health day
_____ Experiencing a life transition	_____ Taking "me" time
_____ Health changes	_____ Going on a vacation or wellness retreat
_____ Holiday or office parties	_____ Spending time in nature
_____ Going to events or places you frequented when drinking	_____ Finishing your to-do list
_____ Being around people who are drinking	_____ Going to recovery meetings
_____ Other: _____	_____ Spending time with loved ones
_____ Other: _____	_____ Spending time with sober folks
_____ Other: _____	_____ Other: _____
_____ Other: _____	_____ Other: _____
	_____ Other: _____
_____ **Total withdrawals**	_____ **Total deposits**

After completing the exercise, are there any situations that are never worth the cost for you? List them here and explain why.

_____

_____

_____

Warning Signs

Sometimes it can be difficult for clients to determine how low their bank account balance is getting. Relapse is sneaky. Clients assume they are doing just fine, and then, all of a sudden, they end up back in a cycle of drinking every night. Helping clients understand their warning signs can help them recognize when they are getting close to overdrafting their account. They'll come to find that the relapse often happens before *the* relapse—which is to say that typically a client's behavior, mood, and thinking change before they even pick up a drink. If they have experienced relapses in the past, unpacking these changes and learning what happened can be incredibly illuminating.

Most warning signs fall into two major categories: engaging in high-risk behaviors associated with hefty withdrawals (e.g., going to bars, spending time with friends who drink) and neglecting self-care by not making enough deposits (e.g., ignoring basic needs, isolating from loved ones). To put it simply, clients are heading toward a relapse when they stop doing things that support their recovery and start engaging in too many behaviors that trigger them. Their mindset changes, and they stop prioritizing their recovery or forget the reasons they were interested in changing their relationship with alcohol in the first place. This leads them to keep their recovery bank account on a very thin margin, where their withdrawals and deposits are barely breaking even, which increases the chance of relapse. A stressor comes along and suddenly they have overdrafted their account. Identifying their warning signs makes it less likely this will happen.

Relapse Warning Signs

Relapses typically don't come out of nowhere. Instead, they are usually preceded by various changes in emotions, thoughts, and behavior that serve as warning signs that your recovery is at risk. Below is a list of common warning sings. Put a check mark by any that you have exhibited before experiencing a relapse.

Changes in Emotions	Changes in Thinking	Changes in Behavior
☐ Denying or avoiding your emotions	☐ Minimizing the consequences of alcohol use	☐ Increase in impulsivity and risky behavior (e.g., saying yes to a party invitation without thinking about if alcohol will be served)
☐ Feeling depressed	☐ Fantasizing about drinking without consequences	
☐ Feeling anxious or restless		☐ Neglecting self-care
☐ Feeling hopeless	☐ Daydreaming about escaping or running away from your problems	☐ Breaking promises to yourself
☐ Increased irritability		☐ Not sleeping enough
☐ Increased feelings of self-pity	☐ Being dishonest with yourself or others	☐ Excessive sleeping
☐ Feeling apathetic about life or your future	☐ Not wanting to prioritize your recovery	☐ Overreacting to situations
		☐ Isolating from others
☐ Feeling angry or having angry outbursts that are disproportionate to the situation (e.g., your boss asks if you can take on another project and you snap at them)	☐ Denying that you have a problem (with alcohol, or anything else you are struggling with)	☐ Hiding things from others
		☐ Canceling important commitments or plans
	☐ Black-and-white thinking (e.g., you have a bad craving and think, This will never get better, I may as well give up now); this type of thinking is often characterized by words like never or always	☐ Skipping work or school
		☐ Rejecting help or support
☐ Increased defensiveness (e.g., if someone asks about your recovery, you shut down or get upset and won't engage in the conversation)		☐ Discontinuing therapy or support groups
		☐ Buying alcohol for others
		☐ Spending time with friends who drink
☐ Feeling uninterested in your recovery		☐ Driving by places you used to drink
		☐ Keeping alcohol in your home or having a stash

Do you notice any patterns in your warning signs? For example, out of the three categories listed, are there certain changes that you tend to experience more than others?

_____

_____

_____

_____

Now pick at least five warnings signs that you identified earlier (making sure there is at least one from each category) and create a plan of what you will do if you experience them.

1. I know my recovery is in trouble when _____ (warning sign).

   Instead, I will _____.

2. I know my recovery is in trouble when _____ (warning sign).

   Instead, I will _____.

3. I know my recovery is in trouble when _____ (warning sign).

   Instead, I will _____.

4. I know my recovery is in trouble when _____ (warning sign).

   Instead, I will _____.

5. I know my recovery is in trouble when _____ (warning sign).

   Instead, I will _____.

Working Through Relapse and Slipups

When clients relapse or slip up, they often feel the need to beat themselves up and call themselves derogatory names. They believe that they must punish themselves to atone for what they've done, as if the crueler they are, the less likely they will be to do it again. This is false. When clients berate themselves, they are literally causing themselves additional stress. And what do most drinkers want to do when they experience stress? Drink! Therefore, punishment and shame only perpetuate the cycle of self-sabotage by triggering clients to drink more. In contrast, it is important to teach clients to treat themselves with compassion and care during these times, much like they would treat a good friend or a small child who was suffering. Although many clients find this approach counterintuitive, when people treat themselves with kindness in times of difficulty, it makes it easier to change and achieve their goals.

According to self-compassion expert Kristin Neff, there are three elements of self-compassion:[43]

1. **Mindfulness:** Instead of getting caught up in their thoughts and feelings, clients simply practice being mindfully and nonjudgmentally aware of how they feel. They can have thoughts, but they are not their thoughts.

2. **Common humanity:** This involves the recognition that everyone is a fallible, imperfect human being. All human beings struggle, and clients are not alone in how they feel.

3. **Self-kindness:** Instead of judging, criticizing, or punishing themselves, clients treat themselves with kindness and care in the face of failure or suffering.

Importantly, self-compassion is not resignation. It does not mean that clients give up on what matters to them or allow themselves to do whatever they want, whenever they want. It does mean they recognize that change is difficult, and they may make mistakes and struggle. However, if clients have struggled with self-criticism for most of their lives, they may need to rebuild trust with themselves. Most of them have changed through self-punishment, or as a reaction to anger or threats from someone else. To create real change, they must be compassionate to and hold themselves accountable at the same time.

Self-Compassion

To help you get into the habit of practicing self-compassion, think about a situation in your life where you made a mistake, didn't achieve a goal, or felt inadequate in some way. This could involve a slipup with drinking or an unrelated experience, such as making a mistake at work, saying something you regret to a friend, or acting out of alignment with your values.

1. Describe the situation here in as much detail as possible. How did you feel at the time?

_____

_____

_____

_____

2. Why was this a difficult situation? Was there an expectation you had of yourself that you didn't meet?

_____

_____

_____

_____

3. How did you talk to yourself after you made this mistake? What phrases or words did you use? How did you feel about yourself? What actions did you end up taking after this experience? For example, did you act out or engage in any unhealthy coping skills?

_____

_____

_____

_____

Now let's work through the experience using self-compassion:

4. Mindfulness: Notice how you felt in the situation and write down what happened in an objective way. Just state the facts without inserting any judgments. If at any point you find yourself engaging in self-judgments for how you dealt with the situation, instead of feeding into the judgment, write down, "I am noticing that I am judging myself for..."

_____

_____

_____

_____

5. Common humanity: If you zoom out and think of the other people in your life, can you imagine how they might have gone through a similar situation? Often, when we judge ourselves, we feel isolated and forget that we are fallible human beings. Are there any unrealistic expectations you have of yourself? Can you see how other people in your position may have made the same mistake as you?

_____

_____

_____

_____

6. Self-kindness: Imagine a friend or loved one of yours is going through the same situation. How would you feel after hearing what they were experiencing? What would you say to them? Would you feel compassion for them? What would you let them know?

_____

_____

_____

_____

7. Compare your answer to the last question with your answer to question #2. Notice how different your responses were and write down any reflections here.

_____

_____

_____

_____

Moderation and Mindful Drinking

Many clients with problematic alcohol use have the goal of moderating their alcohol intake—so they can avoid the consequences of drinking too much—instead of abstaining altogether. Some people can do it, but statistically, it is much easier to quit drinking entirely than to successfully moderate. Remember, alcohol is an addictive substance. Therefore, trying to moderate something that is chemically addictive is going to be inherently difficult, especially if clients have a history of overusing it.

One reason why moderation is so difficult is because it requires clients to constantly make decisions about their alcohol intake—*What? Where? When? How much?*—over and over again. The more decisions they make in a day, even if they are small and mundane, the more exhausted they get, and the more likely they are to make a poor choice. It's also a double whammy in this case. Not only will clients face decision fatigue from moderating, but when they do drink, alcohol impairs their ability to think rationally and carefully weigh their options. It prevents them from being able to think about how their current actions may influence their future, making them more likely to fall back into old patterns. This is why it is so much easier to abstain completely. Clients make one decision and stick with that instead of constantly trying to estimate how they can avoid drinking too much.

The longer a client has been drinking and trying to either quit or cut back will determine how difficult moderation is. This is because the brain literally changes when a habit is created. The more the brain repeats a particular pattern, such as drinking, the deeper this pattern gets ingrained. Think about how bike tire tracks get formed in the mud. The first few times, it can be difficult to ride through the thick sludge, but if someone keeps taking the same path over and over, they are eventually going to leave such a deep groove in the mud that it becomes easier and easier to take the same path. In turn, they keep riding down those same tracks time and time again, and a habit forms.

Now a client can always decide to start forming new habits by putting new tire tracks next to the preexisting one, but that doesn't mean the older pattern just disappears.[44] Those old tire tracks will still be waiting for them, ready to pick up right where they left off. This is part of the reason why drinkers can have success with being abstinent, and then, all of a sudden, they get triggered and fall back into old patterns of behavior. The human brain can change, and people can develop new neural pathways, but just like someone cannot unlearn or forget trauma, the brain doesn't forget how they used alcohol to cope. There is no reset button when it comes to habits.

Habits consist of three parts—a cue, routine, and reward—that together create a habit loop.[45] A cue is a specific trigger that causes the client to crave a specific reward, whether this is a time of day, an emotion, or a location. In turn, the client goes through a specific routine, or a series of actions, to achieve that reward. We all fall into this habit loop. For example, we wake up in the morning, taste our morning breath (cue), and crave the minty taste of our toothpaste (reward), which prompts us to get out of bed and brush our teeth every day (routine). Habits stick because we crave the reward. If we can crave the taste of toothpaste, you can imagine how much more difficult it is to break a habit when the craving involves an artificially pleasurable substance like alcohol.

Unlike toothpaste, alcohol also causes people to need more of the substance over time to experience the same effect, and it dulls the pleasure they get from other enjoyable experiences in their lives. In addition, research shows that when it comes to addictive substances, individuals become hypersensitive to the cues associated with these habits, like seeing the clock strike 5:00 p.m., so they're more likely to reach for that bottle of wine in response to those cues.[46] This hypersensitivity to and affinity for the substance never goes away, even after a period of abstinence. This means that even after someone takes a break from alcohol, their brain will react with the same strong desire to drink as it did when they were at the height of their drinking.[47] Taking a break may reset their tolerance, but it will not change how the brain has learned it should consume alcohol.

If clients do decide to try moderating, my recommendation is that they abstain from alcohol for at least 30 days. At this point, you might be wondering, *What's the point of having them quit for 30 days if they aren't resetting their brain?* Old habits may never truly disappear, but clients still have an opportunity to create new habits that give them a shot at doing something different. By repeating these new habits over time, clients can create new neural pathways in the brain that reinforce the experience of sobriety. For example, if every time a client feels stressed, they call a friend or take a hot bath instead of turning to alcohol, they are rewiring their brain. The same process occurs when clients practice socializing sober or go on a date without drinking alcohol to quell their nerves. Thirty days of practicing a new habit will not be as deeply ingrained as years of drinking, but it's a great start that can give clients a chance to do something different.

Can You Moderate?

When it comes to changing your relationship with alcohol, you can try to moderate your use or quit altogether. However, for most people, it is much easier to just stop drinking than it is to temper their use. To see if moderation is possible for you, answer the following questions. Be sure to answer honestly. This quiz will not be accurate if you are dishonest. If you notice yourself exaggerating the truth or trying to justify why you don't meet a certain criterion, this is a very good sign that you need to explore this further.

_____ 1. Have you ever been physically addicted to alcohol, meaning that you experienced withdrawals when you stopped?

Yes (+5)   No (0)

_____ 2. Do you have anxiety, depression, or another mental health issue?

Yes (+2)   No (0)

_____ 3. Do you use alcohol to deal with stress?

Yes (+1)   No (0)

_____ 4. Do you have a history of trauma or PTSD?

Yes (+2)   No (0)

_____ 5. Do you drink alone?

Yes (+2)   No (0)

_____ 6. Is it common for you to black out while drinking?

Yes (+3)   No (0)

_____ 7. Do you use alcohol to deal with social anxiety?

Yes (+2)   No (0)

_____ 8. Are your close friends, your spouse, your immediate family, or the people you spend a lot of time with moderate to heavy drinkers?

Yes (+2)   No (0)

_____ 9. Do you have hobbies or interests outside of drinking?

Yes (−1)   No (0)

_____ 10. Were you raised in an environment where there was heavy drinking?

Yes (+2)   No (0)

_____ 11. Is there a history of substance use issues in your family?

Yes (+2)   No (0)

_____ 12. Have you encountered legal, probationary, school, or work trouble because of your drinking?

Yes (+3)   No (0)

_____ 13. Do you have an eating disorder or a history of one?

Yes (+1)   No (0)

_____ 14. Do you have a history of using other non-prescribed substances?

Yes (+1)   No (0)

_____ 15. Was your first drink before the age of 15?

Yes (+1)   No (0)

_____ 16. Has your drinking negatively impacted your relationships or loved ones?

Yes (+2)   No (0)

_____ 17. Do you drink every day?

Yes (+2)   No (0)

_____ 18. Do you have any medical issues?

Yes (+2)   No (0)

_____ 19. Are you a binge drinker?

Yes (+2)   No (0)

_____ 20. Have you been to an inpatient facility or detox center for drinking?

Yes (+3)   No (0)

_____ 21. Has your alcohol use been increasing to get the same effect?

Yes (+2)   No (0)

_____ 22. When you drink, do you have a hard time stopping?

Yes (+3)   No (0)

_____ 23. Have you tried to cut back on drinking and been unable to?

Yes (+2)   No (0)

_____ 24. Have you lost interest in your regular hobbies or blown off commitments or friends so you can continue drinking?

Yes (+2)   No (0)

_____ 25. Do you experience feelings of shame or guilt due to drinking?

Yes (+1)   No (0)

_____ 26. Do you have a group of supportive people in your life you can rely on?

Yes (−2)   No (0)

_____ 27. Do you have people in your life with whom you can do things that don't involve drinking?

Yes (−1)   No (0)

_____ 28. Are you willing to tell people in your life you want to cut back on drinking so they can support you?

Yes (−2)   No (0)

To calculate your total score, add up your answers, making sure to subtract any points from your score that have a minus sign.

Total score: _____

Scoring Key

9 and below: You may be able to successfully moderate your drinking. You have the best shot of making this work by increasing your coping skills, working on your mental health, and being intentional about the times you choose to drink.

10–30: It's unlikely that you will be able to effectively moderate. You may be able to do it for periods of time, but it will likely be based on willpower, and you will slip back into old patterns. If you do not want to become abstinent, you will likely always fall back into drinking too much. Your alcohol use could stay the same or it could continue to get worse, and you could eventually advance to a score over 30.

31–50: It is extremely unlikely you will be able to successfully moderate. Even if you do work on yourself and heal some of the deeper issues causing you to drink, your drinking has progressed to the point where that habit is so worn down, it will be nearly impossible to moderate.

What was it like answering the questions from the quiz?

_____

_____

_____

_____

After reading through the scoring information, how do you feel about the score you received?

_____

_____

_____

_____

Mindful Drinking

For many clients looking to change their relationship with alcohol, their goal is often to practice mindful drinking, in which they are more intentional about the drinks they choose to consume. Although it can be tempting for clients to cut back their drinking instead of quitting altogether, unlike other habits—where it's more effective to start small and build from there—it can be more effective to take a break from alcohol before trying to moderate. That's because alcohol is an addictive substance that significantly affects mental and physical health. As a result, if clients simply try to cut back, they may not experience any of the positive benefits of how they feel without alcohol. Alcohol takes some time to completely leave their system, especially if they have been drinking a lot or for a long time.

Whether someone wants to moderate their use or quit completely, start with the goal of not drinking for 30 days. The idea of forever can be extremely overwhelming. If 30 days is too long, start with 5, 7, or 10 days, and go from there. If 30 days goes well, see if they can do another 30. Maybe another. There is a legitimate reason why AA talks about taking things one day at a time. Clients don't have to plan for the rest of their lives. They can experiment and see what works for them.

However, in my experience, if someone struggles to take a 30-day break from alcohol, it's unlikely they will be able to successfully moderate. I have also found that clients have the best shot of successfully moderating if they take at least four months off from drinking. This does not include any time spent in a facility like rehab or jail. This amount of time will usually allow them to experience and cope with triggers, get through some holidays, create new habits, deal with the emotional challenges of being sober, and experience a change in their lifestyle if needed. Cravings will also dramatically decrease after 120 days. After taking a break, here are a few important tips that clients can use to make moderation more effective:

Plan the drink at least 24 hours in advance. This will ensure clients are drinking because they want to, rather than in response to a trigger. As Roy Baumeister says, "The best decision makers are the ones who know when *not* to trust themselves."[48] If they wait 24 hours, they can more clearly evaluate if they truly want a drink or are just drinking as a knee-jerk reaction to something. Along similar lines, it can be helpful for them to not keep alcohol at home. It is easy to fall into a habit when alcohol is readily available. If clients have to seek out alcohol by buying it, that is another step they must go through.

Create a plan. To have a shot at moderating effectively, it is incredibly important that clients create a plan before they start drinking. Once they have their first drink, it is hard to make good decisions because their prefrontal cortex goes offline. If clients do not have a plan going into the situation, understand that no plan is a plan to drink. "Maybe I will drink" doesn't cut it. If possible, encourage clients to make a plan that applies to all situations. For example, they can decide they will never have more than two drinks, not drink more than two nights a week, never take shots, or never drink when they are upset. This can help reduce decision fatigue since they stick to one plan rather than constantly questioning what they will do in each situation.

Avoid using alcohol to cope with emotions. Not only is drinking an ineffective way to process emotions, but when clients are in an emotional state, it is going to be even more difficult for them to moderate. If they choose to drink, they should plan it out in advance and make it a deliberate choice so they can savor the experience and be mindful of how it feels.

Do not drink alone. Drinking alone can become a slippery slope. Without anyone there, it can be easy for clients to get carried away and forget the promises they made to themselves. Accountability is incredibly important if they are trying to moderate because, left to their own devices, it can be easy to fall into old patterns.

Rely on support. Connection and accountability are important if someone is trying to stay sober, but this is also true for those moderating. Once clients have one drink, it is more difficult for them to stick to their commitments. Having people in their lives who know about their intention to cut back on alcohol can give them an extra layer of accountability. The most powerful form of accountability involves only drinking in the presence of another person who is aware that the client's goal is to have no more than one glass or to not get drunk. If that is not an option, clients can also let someone else know about their plans.

Replace alcoholic beverages with a nonalcoholic swap. Alcohol can make an ordinary day or evening feel special, which is why people often use alcohol to mark the end of the day or week. It allows them to experience the enjoyment of sipping on something different than they did during the day, which is where nonalcoholic beverages can be a helpful swap. Making a mocktail on a Friday night can replace a client's cocktail ritual and make them feel like they are drinking something different and special. Sober bars are popping up around the country, and more restaurants are serving mocktails than ever. Alcohol-free beer, wine, and spirits have also come a long way. Some are meant to taste like alcohol, such as zero-proof tequila or beer, while others are meant to taste dry or tart but not mimic the taste of alcohol.

If someone is sober curious or interested in moderating, alcohol-free beverages are an obvious support. However, for people who want or need to stop drinking completely, alcohol-free beverages can be triggering, especially the ones that mimic the taste of alcohol. Some nonalcoholic beverages also contain small traces of alcohol (0.05 percent ABV), so groups that are strictly abstinence-based may not consider this sobriety. If someone falls on the moderate-to-severe end of the alcohol use spectrum, it may benefit them to abstain from these drinks for the first few months of sobriety until they are more secure. Intentions also matter. If someone starts drinking alcohol-free beverages in a way that seems compulsive or in increasing amounts, this is a sign they should abstain for a while until their recovery is stronger. Similarly, if someone starts drinking excessive amounts of kombucha (which has a very low percentage of alcohol) in attempts to feel a buzz, these beverages are not healthy for them right now.

Accept that there is no moderation when drunk. Moderation is only effective if clients are willing to keep their blood alcohol content (BAC) below a certain point. It is unrealistic for them to have the goal of getting drunk enough to have fun and party, but not so drunk that there are negative consequences. Once their BAC hits 0.06 and above, clients are impaired and do not have good judgment. Their reasoning and willpower are impaired. Every person needs to consume a different number of drinks to reach this BAC level, depending on weight and the amount of food they ate before drinking. For women, this is one to two drinks per hour, while for men, it's two to three drinks. BAC lowers .015 per hour. If moderating is important to a client, you may want to encourage them to get a breathalyzer or use an online BAC calculator. However, this takes a lot of effort, and it's worth noting that if someone needs to spend a large amount of time trying to control their drinking, it is unlikely they will be able to effectively moderate over the long term. Willpower can only get them so far before they run out of energy and slip into old habits.

Pace the drinking. It takes anywhere between 5 and 20 minutes to start feeling the effects of one alcoholic beverage. If clients drink too quickly, it can be difficult to pace themselves, and they can end up drinking more than intended. A good rule of thumb is for clients to drink one nonalcoholic beverage after every alcoholic beverage to slow down their consumption. Alcohol is dehydrating. Sometimes when clients reach for another drink, they are thirsty. Drinking enough water before, during, and after consuming alcohol can help them moderate. It is also important to make sure they don't drink on an empty stomach since this increases the rate of impairment.

Practice mindfulness. It may be tempting for clients to celebrate making it 120 days without alcohol by going out and drinking whatever they want. However, this is a recipe for falling right back into their old patterns. Instead, it is helpful for their first post-break drink to be a mindful experience so they can fully appreciate how it feels compared to being sober for a few months. Encourage clients to stick to one drink for this exercise so they can experience exactly how alcohol feels as it enters their system, as they start feeling its effects, and as it leaves. Clients will be able to recognize if they want another drink by judging how they feel before, during, and after they consume alcohol.

Be willing to compromise. Some situations will not work for moderation, no matter how hard clients try. Sometimes clients have too much history with overdrinking a certain type of alcoholic beverage, like margaritas, which makes moderation out of the question. Or maybe they have an old drinking buddy with whom they always drink too much, and no matter how much clients say no to another drink, they always succumb to the pressure with this person. Or maybe they simply cannot go to Las Vegas without blacking out. Clients must be willing to stay sober in these situations or to avoid engaging in these situations altogether. It is important to be honest with themselves about their limits so they can make thoughtful decisions. Furthermore, alcohol is addictive, and given the right circumstances, anyone can escalate in their drinking behaviors to the point where they have a severe substance use issue. Addiction can sneak up quickly, especially if clients have a history of using alcohol in unhealthy ways in the past. Moderation requires constant vigilance.

Mindful Drinking Exercise

After taking at least 30 days off from drinking, engage in this mindful drinking exercise so you can learn more about how your body and mind react to alcohol. As tempting as it is to want to celebrate your abstinence by getting drunk, this exercise will be much more effective if you do it after a break from alcohol, rather than waiting to fall back into old patterns. This exercise will take about one hour of your time. Decide what alcoholic beverage you are going to have in advance. You don't have to do this exercise alone, but it is important to do it in a way that you can be mindful of how you are feeling and to allow yourself time to take notes throughout. Trying to do this while you are out to dinner with a friend is unlikely to be effective.

1. What are you going to be drinking for this exercise? _____

2. How do you feel right now, before drinking any alcohol? Eager? Impatient? Anxious?

   _____

   _____

   _____

3. Prepare the beverage you plan to drink. Be mindful of the sights and smells as you go through the process. For example, if it is a canned beverage, notice how the can feels in your hand. Listen as you crack it open. If it is a bottle of wine, notice how it feels to uncork the bottle and how it sounds as you pour the wine into a glass. If it is a mixed drink, be mindful as you go through each stage of preparation, pausing to take in the sights and smells. Many individuals experience pleasure or stress relief (as if they already had a drink) before they even take a sip. Did this happen to you? Write down your observations below. Was it difficult to take your time? What was it like to mindfully prepare to drink?

   _____

   _____

   _____

4. Take a deep breath and smell the beverage as you pick it up. Notice how it looks and feels in your hand. Now start drinking. Sip very slowly. Notice the taste. Notice how the liquid feels in your mouth. Is it bubbly? Soft? Does it burn going down your throat? Does it feel warm when it hits your belly? Notice everything. Write down your observations here.

_____

_____

_____

5. Most alcoholic beverages take anywhere between 5 to 20 minutes to kick in. As you drink, notice how, or if, your mood or thoughts start to change. Notice the moment when you start to feel the effects of alcohol. How does it feel?

_____

_____

_____

6. Continue to drink the beverage slowly. Spend at least 30 minutes drinking your beverage. Notice if you want to drink it faster. Take occasional moments to pause while you're drinking and write down any thoughts that come up below.

_____

_____

_____

7. After you finish drinking your beverage, how do you feel? Do you want another one? Are you frustrated that you are doing this exercise? Notice any thoughts, emotions, or sensations that you have.

_____

_____

_____

8. Sit for 15 minutes and notice how it feels to be under the influence of one drink. What sensations, thoughts, or emotions are you having? As the alcohol starts to wear off, how do you feel? What is this experience like for you?

_____

_____

_____

9. Wait one hour from when you first started drinking for the alcohol to leave your system. How do you feel now? Is there anything you notice? Was the experience as good as you expected? Did you have more enjoyment planning it than doing it?

_____

_____

_____

10. After considering how this experience was for you, is having one drink worth it for you? Is drinking worth it? Could a mocktail or nonalcoholic beverage do the trick instead?

_____

_____

_____

11. Be mindful of your thoughts and emotions tomorrow. Notice if you have any cravings for alcohol that you didn't during your break from drinking. Write down any reflections here.

_____

_____

_____

Is Moderating Working?

If you have been moderating for a few months and continue to slip up or drink more than you'd like, this worksheet will help you understand what's going on and how to make changes. Pick a recent scenario where you drank more than you wanted to or felt like you were not able to successfully moderate, then answer the following questions about the experience.

Date of relapse or slipup: _____

1. Describe what happened. Where were you when you relapsed? Who were you with? How much did you drink? What were you doing? What were others doing?

_____

_____

_____

_____

2. How were you feeling right before you picked up the drink?

_____

_____

_____

_____

3. How were you feeling earlier in the day or in the past week?

_____

_____

_____

_____

4. How did you feel after you took the first drink? The second? The third? How did you feel when you were done drinking? If your feelings changed, describe what you were feeling like after a few hours, the next day, the next week, or the next month.

_____

_____

_____

5. How much time passed between when you started thinking about drinking and when you actually started drinking? When did you decide that you were going to drink? Was it planned? Spontaneous?

_____

_____

_____

6. Did you experience any cravings or urges? If yes, did you engage in urge surfing? Did you attempt to use any coping skills? Did you reach out for support or call anyone? Did you do anything to take care of yourself that day? If not, what stopped you?

_____

_____

_____

7. Did you think about what would happen after you drank? Did you try to imagine how this relapse would impact your future and your life as a way to try to deter yourself from drinking? (This is known as playing the tape through). If not, why?

_____

_____

_____

8. When was the point where you lost control or were unable to moderate your drinking?

_____

_____

_____

9. Did you try to stop yourself from drinking more after the first drink?

_____

_____

_____

10. Did you take any actions that were out of alignment with your values while drunk? Were there any negative consequences to your behavior?

_____

_____

_____

11. Was this experience worth it? Would you do it again knowing what you know now?

_____

_____

_____

12. What is working? What isn't working? List out any coping skills, habits, beliefs, or actions that are either helping or interfering with your ability to moderate.

What are you doing that is helping you moderate?	What habits are preventing you from being able to moderate?

Nothing changes if nothing changes. After completing the exercise, what are at least three things that you will do differently next time?

_____

_____

_____

References

For your convenience, purchasers can download and print the worksheets from www.pesi.com/NDTWorkbook

1 SAMHSA's Center for Behavioral Health Statistics and Quality, "2019 National Survey on Drug Use and Health, Table 2.20B—Binge Alcohol Use in Past Month among Persons Aged 12 or Older, by Age Group and Demographic Characteristics: Percentages, 2018 and 2019," https://www.samhsa.gov/data/sites /default/files/reports/rpt29394/NSDUHDetailedTabs2019/NSDUHDetTabsSect2pe2019.htm#tab2-20b.

2 Jonathan Chick, "Alcohol and COVID-19," *Alcohol and Alcoholism* 55, no. 4 (2020): 341–342, https://doi.org/10.1093/alcalc/agaa039.

3 GBD 2016 Alcohol Collaborators, "Alcohol Use and Burden for 195 Countries and Territories, 1990– 2016: A Systematic Analysis for the Global Burden of Disease Study 2016," *The Lancet* 392, no. 10152 (September 22, 2018): 1015–1035, https://doi.org/10.1016/S0140-6736(18)31310-2.

4 Samir Zahkari, "Overview: How Is Alcohol Metabolized by the Body?" *Alcohol Research & Health* 29, no. 4 (2006): 245–254.

5 Clair R. Martin, Vadim Osadchiy, Amir Kalani, and Emeran A. Mayer, "The Brain-Gut-Microbiome Axis," *Cellular and Molecular Gastroenterology and Hepatology* 6, no. 2 (2018): 133–148.

6 Jennifer L. Steiner, Kristen T. Crowell, and Charles H. Lang, "Impact of Alcohol on Glycemic Control and Insulin Action," *Biomolecules* 5, no 4 (2015): 2223–2246.

7 Zahkari, "How Is Alcohol Metabolized?"

8 Helmut K. Seitz and Felix Stickel, "Acetaldehyde as an Underestimated Risk Factor for Cancer Development: Role of Genetics in Ethanol Metabolism," *Genes & Nutrition* 5, no. 2 (June 5, 2010): 121–128.

9 Peter Boyle and Paolo Boffetta, "Alcohol Consumption and Breast Cancer Risk," *Breast Cancer Research* 11, S3 (2009), https://doi.org/10.1186/bcr2422.

10 Rui Guo and Jun Ren, "Alcohol and Acetaldehyde in Public Health: From Marvel to Menace," *International Journal of Environmental Research and Public Health* 7, no. 4 (2010): 1285–1301, https://doi.org/10.3390 /ijerph7041285.

11 Matthew P. Walker, *Why We Sleep: The New Science of Sleep and Dreams* (New York: Scribner, 2017).

12 Anya Topiwala, Klaus P. Ebmeier, Thomas Maullin-Sapey, and Thomas E. Nichols, "No Safe Level of Alcohol Consumption for Brain Health: Observational Cohort Study of 25,378 UK Biobank Participants" (unpublished manuscript, May 12, 2021), https://doi.org/10.1101/2021.05.10.21256931.

13 Natalie Grover, "Any Amount of Alcohol Consumption Is Harmful to the Brain, Finds Study," *The Guardian*, May 18, 2021, https://www.theguardian.com/society/2021/may/18/any-amount-of-alcohol -consumption-harmful-to-the-brain-finds-study.

14 George F. Koob et al., "Addiction as a Stress Surfeit Disorder," *Neuropharmacology* 76, part B (2014): 370–382.

15 Nora D. Volkow and Marisela Morales, "The Brain on Drugs: From Reward to Addiction," *Cell* 162, no. 4 (2015): 712–725, https://doi.org/10.1016/j.cell.2015.07.046.

16 Judith Grisel, *Never Enough: The Neuroscience and Experience of Addiction* (New York: Anchor Books, 2018).

17 Elizabeth Stanley, *Widen the Window: Training Your Brain and Body to Thrive During Stress and Recover from Trauma* (New York: Avery, 2019). The idea that stress and trauma are on the same continuum is credited to Elizabeth Stanley and discussed in her book.

18 Ibid.

19 Daniel J. Siegel, *The Developing Mind: Toward a Neurobiology of Interpersonal Experience* (Guilford Press, 1999).

20 Brené Brown, *I Thought It Was Just Me (but It Isn't): Making the Journey from "What Will People Think?" to "I Am Enough"* (New York: Avery, 2018).

21 Bessel van der Kolk, *The Body Keeps the Score* (New York: Penguin Books, 2015).

22 Brené Brown, *Daring Greatly: How the Courage to Be Vulnerable Transforms the Way We Live, Love, Parent, and Lead* (New York: Avery, 2015).

23 Ibid. Texas professor James Pennbaker studied rape and incest survivors and what happens when they keep their experiences a secret. Brené Brown cited this research in her book.

24 Bruce D. Perry and Maia Szalavitz, *The Boy Who was Raised as a Dog and Other Stories from a Child Psychiatrist's Notebook: What Traumatized Children Can Teach Us About Loss, Love, and Healing* (New York: Basic Books, 2008).

25 Marc Brackett, *Permission to Feel: Unlocking the Power of Emotions to Help Our Kids, Ourselves, and Our Society Thrive* (New York: Celadon Books, 2019).

26 Lisa Feldman Barrett, *How Emotions Are Made: The Secret Life of the Brain* (Boston: Houghton Mifflin Harcourt, 2017).

27 Ibid.

28 David Robson, "There Really Are 50 Eskimo Words for 'Snow,'" *The Washington Post*, January 14, 2013.

29 Sabrina Stierwalt, "Why Do We Laugh?" *Scientific American*, February 9, 2020, https://www.scientificamerican.com/article/why-do-we-laugh.

30 Jane Brody, "Biological Role of Emotional Tears Emerges Through Recent Studies," *The New York Times*, August 31, 1982.

31 Fariha Roisin, "Natural Wine Is My Self-Care," *The New York Times*, June 3, 2019.

32 A. H. Maslow, "A Theory of Human Motivation," *Psychological Review* 50, no. 4 (1943): 430–437.

33 Scott Barry Kaufman, *Transcend: The New Science of Self-Actualization* (New York: Tarcher Perigee, 2020).

34 Jeffrey A. Hall, "How Many Hours Does It Take to Make a Friend?" *Journal of Social and Personal Relationships*, March 15, 2018.

35 Ibid.

36 Gillian M. Sandstrom and Elizabeth W. Dunn, "Social Interactions and Well-Being: The Surprising Power of Weak Ties," *Personality and Social Psychology Bulletin* 40, no. 7 (July 2014): 910–922, https://doi.org/10.1177/0146167214529799.

37 "The Myth of Beer Goggles?" *Discover Magazine*, August 20, 2015, https://www.discovermagazine.com /mind/the-myth-of-beer-goggles.

38 William H. George et al., "Women's Sexual Arousal: Effects of High Alcohol Dosages and Self-Control Instructions," *Hormones and Behavior* 59, no. 5 (March 23, 2011): 730–738, https://doi.org/10.1016 /j.yhbeh.2011.03.006.

39 Emily Nagoski, *Come as You Are: The Surprising New Science That Will Transform Your Sex Life* (New York: Simon & Schuster Paperbacks, 2021).

40 Ibid.

41 Ibid.

42 Holly Whitaker, *Quit Like a Woman: The Radical Choice to Not Drink in a Culture Obsessed with Alcohol* (New York: Dial Press, 2020).

43 Kristin Neff, *Self-Compassion: The Proven Power of Being Kind to Yourself* (New York: HarperCollins, 2011).

44 Marc D. Lewis, *The Biology of Desire: Why Addiction Is Not a Disease* (New York: Public Affairs, 2018).

45 Charles Duhigg, *The Power of Habit: Why We Do What We Do in Life and Business* (New York: Random House, 2014).

46 Kent C. Berridge and Terry E. Robinson, "Liking, Wanting, and the Incentive-Sensitization Theory of Addiction," *American Psychologist* 71, no. 8 (2016): 670–679, https://doi.org/10.1037/amp0000059.

47 Ibid.

48 Roy F. Baumeister and John Tierney, *Willpower: Rediscovering the Greatest Human Strength* (London: Penguin, 2012).

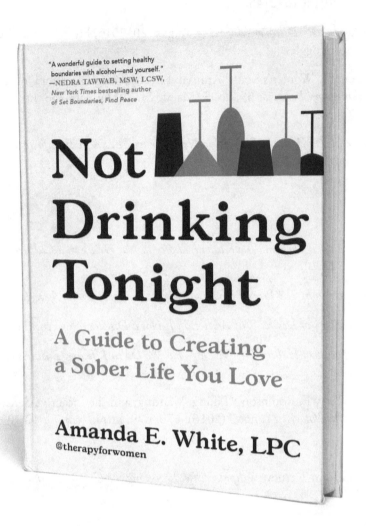

To learn more about Amanda White's
work and program, read her first book
Not Drinking Tonight
AVAILABLE EVERYWHERE

hachette
BOOKS